LESSON PLAN

LESSON PLAN

An Agenda for Change in
American Higher Education

William G. Bowen
and Michael S. McPherson

PRINCETON UNIVERSITY PRESS

Princeton and Oxford

press.princeton.edu

Jacket design by Faceout Studio

Library of Congress Cataloging-in-Publication Data
Names: Bowen, William G., author. | McPherson, Michael
S., author.
Title: An agenda for change in American higher education /
William G. Bowen and Michael S. McPherson.
Description: Princeton, New Jersey : Princeton University
Press, 2016. | Includes bibliographical references and index.
Identifiers: LCCN 2015042668| ISBN 9780691172101
(hardcover : alk. paper) |
ISBN 0691172102 (hardcover : alk. paper)
Subjects: LCSH: Education, Higher—United States. |
Education, Higher—Aims and objectives.
Classification: LCC LA227.4 .B685 2016 | DDC 378.73—
dc23 LC record available at http://lccn.loc.gov/2015042668

British Library Cataloging-in-Publication Data is available

This book has been composed in Minion Pro

Printed on acid-free paper. ∞

Printed in the United States of America

10 9 8 7 6 5 4 3 2 1

Contents

Preface and Acknowledgments

We have been motivated to write this short book because of our conviction that American higher education, for all of its accomplishments, needs to do much better than it is doing at present in meeting pressing national needs, especially achieving higher levels of educational attainment at the undergraduate level and reducing what are now marked disparities in outcomes related to socioeconomic status. Controlling costs is also essential.

As the Organisation for Economic Co-operation and Development (OECD) has shown, American higher education has lost its premier place in the league tables of educational attainment and lags behind other countries in moving ahead. Moreover, it is a cruel fact that higher education in America, once seen as the engine of social mobility in a land of opportunity, now serves at times, however inadvertently, to perpetuate gaps in outcomes related to socioeconomic status. This is the result of many forces. These include the high correlation between family circumstances and the ability of young people to assemble portfolios of achievement that appeal to admissions directors seeking to build prestigious classes of excellent students. Also at play is a combination of rising net tuition costs at public institutions hard hit by state funding cutbacks and financial aid systems that too often reward "merit" rather than meet need. Finally, there is the deadening effect of too much poor teaching of foundational courses in fields such as mathematics; the associated high levels of attrition, especially among less well-prepared students, are a leading cause of disparities in outcomes. Methods of teaching in specific parts of American higher education need to be altered to improve educational outcomes and control (reduce?) costs of instruction.

These are serious problems. But it is also true that many of the so-called crises in higher education are overblown. Specific examples, which we discuss at some length in this book, are alleged "administrative bloat" and "mountains" of student debt. Exaggerating these concerns, if not misstating the facts entirely, only complicates and confuses discussions of how to make progress in confronting the all-too-real challenges facing higher education.

We certainly do not claim that improvements in higher education are a panacea for addressing the present-day failings of education in America, which include, most notably, the unequal educational opportunities that plague children from disadvantaged families from their earliest days. The reality of these failings, and the urgent need to address them, cannot, however, serve as an excuse for higher education to do less than its best.

Nor can we claim that, overall, the content of this book represents extensive original research. It does not. Instead it is, in the main, our attempt to collect together, in one place and in a document of manageable size, what is known and what can be inferred about the current "facts of life" in American higher education. We attempt to be both reasonably comprehensive and reasonably concise, but not, we hope, at the expense of getting basic points wrong. We are reminded of the Einstein aphorism "Everything should be made as simple as possible, but not more so."

In the process of distinguishing fact from fiction, we seek to identify the most promising ways of pushing ahead. Work on other projects has persuaded us, however, that a realistic recognition of where we are today is a necessary precursor to real progress. Short of an honest stocktaking, it will be impossible to muster the will—on the part of faculty, administrators, trustees, and legislators—to undertake a needed re-engineering of essential elements of undergraduate instruction (by no means all elements, but certainly some). It can be too easy to assume either that all is well or that tinkering around the edges is all that is required. Still, this is definitely not a narrative of despair. Our discussion of an "agenda for change" highlights the many opportunities for progress.

In concluding this preface, we should explain what may seem an odd emphasis, at some places in the text, on the recent histories of Sweet Briar College in Virginia, Cooper Union in New York, and colleges and universities in Virginia that have had to cope with cutbacks in state funding. We believe that each of these "institutional sagas" has broader lessons for higher education; and, concurrently with working on this book, we spent time exploring these lessons.[1] These instances of struggle at the

[1] Readers interested in the (to us) fascinating sagas of Sweet Briar and Cooper Union may want to read the separate Ithaka S+R "issue brief" by Lawrence S. Bacow and Bowen titled "Double Trouble: Sweet Briar College and Cooper Union," September 21, 2015, available at www.sr.ithaka.org/blog/double-trouble/. (ITHAKA is a nonprofit entity that is the parent of JSTOR and Portico and that also has a research arm.) The *Chronicle of Higher Education* has published an abridged versions of our thinking on these two cases, "The Painful Lessons of Sweet Briar and Cooper Union," September 24, 2015, available at http://chronicle.com/article/The-Painful -Lessons-of-Sweet/233369/. Readers interested in the rich detail of the Virginia story should consult the long account of a careful econometric study carried out by staff

institutional level also serve to put some "flesh on the bone" of the broader analysis.

Acknowledgments

Our manifold debts to other scholars are referenced in the text and in the numerous footnotes. Here we thank more fully Sandy Baum, senior fellow at the Urban Institute, and Sarah E. Turner, chair of the Department of Economics at the University of Virginia. Sandy has provided both much data, of which she is the unquestioned master, and countless good ideas. Sarah has patiently read much of the manuscript with a critical eye and made many suggestions for improvements—not all of which we could accept, given the constraints imposed by our determination to write (for once!) a short book.

Among the many other scholars and leaders of higher education who have played big roles in the evolution and sharpening of our thinking, we must mention especially Rebecca Blank at the University of Wisconsin, Brian Rosenberg at Macalester College, John Hennessy and Candace Thille at Stanford University, Alexandra Logue at the City University of New York, William E. Kirwan of the University System of Maryland, Nancy Zimpher at the State University of New York, and Daphne Koller at Coursera.

We also thank our principal colleagues and assistants, who contributed in ways too numerous to catalog: at the Spencer Foundation, Charles Kurose and Esperanza Johnson; at ITHAKA,

---

at Ithaka S+R. For a detailed description, see Christine Mulhern, Richard R. Spies, Matthew P. Staiger, and D. Derek Wu, "The Effects of Rising Student Costs in Higher Education: Evidence from Public Institutions in Virginia," March 4, 2015, available at http://sr.ithaka.org/research-publications/effects-rising-student-costs-higher -education. This research was carried out by the research arm of ITHAKA (Ithaka S+R) in close collaboration with the State Council of Higher Education in Virginia (SCHEV), led by Peter Blake.

Kevin Guthrie, Deanna Marcum, Martin Kurzweil, Lisa Krueger, Suzanne Pichler, Kathy Patterson, and especially Johanna Brownell. Johanna deserves special recognition for having filled in many holes and tirelessly edited the entire manuscript. More generally, the Spencer Foundation and ITHAKA have supported this project in countless ways throughout its gestation; this book is, then, a product of what we are pleased to regard as joint sponsorship.

Our relationship with the Princeton University Press has been exemplary in every way. The director, Peter J. Dougherty, took a personal interest in this book from the start. Peter did his best to keep us focused on the crucial questions and to leave to others trips down innumerable tributaries of the main stream. The entire team at the Princeton University Press broke all records in managing the process of transforming a manuscript into a book; we are grateful to all of them.

We should also note that, as the numerous cites and cross-references will show, this book builds directly on two prior publications of the Princeton University Press. *Crossing the Finish Line: Completing College in America's Public Universities* (by Bowen, Matthew M. Chingos, and McPherson) spared us the need to go over masses of detail concerning completion rates. The other book, *Locus of Authority: The Evolution of Faculty Governance in American Higher Education* (by Bowen and Eugene M. Tobin of The Andrew W. Mellon Foundation, published jointly with ITHAKA), discusses extensively the need for changes, some subtle, in established notions of "shared governance" that are essential to the successful pursuit of much of the agenda for change discussed in the last part of the book.

The collaboration of the two authors has been deeply satisfying to both of us. Whatever faults remain (and we are of course fully responsible for them), this book is, we believe, much better that what either of us could have produced alone.

Finally, we express far more than perfunctory thanks to our wives, Sandy Baum and Mary Ellen Bowen, for their exceptional patience with us during hectic days.

William G. Bowen
Michael S. McPherson
January 2016

LESSON PLAN

PART I

Prelude

Tempting as it always is to put the best possible face on most everything, there are times for candid and forceful self-appraisals. It is in that spirit that we offer our sense of the all-too-limited success that American higher education is having today in meeting pressing national needs (its great accomplishments notwithstanding). It is also true, as we have said in the preface, that public discussion often exaggerates, if it does not misstate entirely, issues that lend themselves to hyperbole.

There is no denying the fact that our country faces pressing needs. These include achieving higher levels of educational attainment, in large part by raising stagnant completion rates, reducing long time-to-degree, reversing unacceptable disparities in outcomes related to socioeconomic status, and responsibly addressing concerns about affordability that have been driven by both cutbacks in government support and the limited success of higher education in finding effective ways of reducing costs while maintaining educational quality. Disparities in outcomes by socioeconomic status are, of course, serious matters in their own right in a country that supposedly puts a high value on social mobility and should be genuinely concerned about opportunity for all. Moreover, we do not think aspirations for higher levels of educational attainment overall can be satisfied without substantial progress in meeting the educational needs of students from low-income and otherwise disadvantaged families.

Organization of the Book

In part I (this prelude) we provide a framework for thinking about the issues before us.

In part II we assemble as much evidence as we can to document the seriousness of these interconnected issues—which too many in higher education seem reluctant to acknowledge, much less attack effectively. William "Brit" Kirwan, who recently retired as chancellor of the University System of Maryland, shares this concern. In an "exit" interview, he observed: "All of higher education, maybe with a few exceptions [the extremely well-endowed private institutions], is going to be in for a very difficult time in the coming decade. University leaders and boards are not doing enough to come to grips with what universities will be facing in the coming years."[1] We agree. We believe that leadership, at both administrative and board levels, is too often reluctant to consider the major changes—in teaching methods, for example—needed to improve how instruction is delivered and how costs are controlled. There is also much room for progress in deciding how student aid funds are allocated.

In part III we discuss an "agenda for change"—approaches to consider in the search for ways to ameliorate, if not solve, these

[1] Kellie Woodhouse, "A Career's Worth of Change," *Inside Higher Ed*, July 14, 2015, available at https://www.insidehighered.com/news/2015/07/14/exit-interview-outgoing-university-system-maryland-chancellor-brit-kirwan.

problems. Faculty, no less than administrators and trustees, need to be apprised of these challenges; they need to become active participants in finding educationally and financially responsible solutions. There is much that can be accomplished. Alexis de Tocqueville, in his famous *Democracy in America* (1835), observed: "The greatness of America lies not in being more enlightened than any other nation, but rather in her ability to repair her faults."[2] However true this may have been in the early part of the nineteenth century, we fervently hope that it is true today.

Framework for Analysis

It is useful to begin by describing the general framework within which we are thinking. The higher education system is a means of investing in human capital or, more ambitiously, in human improvement. Like any investment, investment in human capital involves paying present costs to gain future benefits. The most important resource here is the time of the students themselves, who need to devote sustained effort to the process of acquiring new skills and learning new things. Student time can be used most effectively when it is complemented with other resources—teachers and facilities—that can make learning opportunities more effective.

There is probably no better-documented finding in the social sciences than that education pays. Studies across a wide variety of countries, with differing economic systems, examining different levels of education and employing a range of statistical techniques, have shown with mind-numbing consistency that the earnings differential between people with more education versus

[2] Alexis de Tocqueville, *Democracy in America*, vol. 1, chapter 8.

those with less education more than compensates students for the investment in time and money they make (or society makes on their behalf) in becoming more educated.[3]

Impressive as the data collection efforts and analytical advances underlying these studies have been, to us the most persuasive evidence of the persistent high value of investments in education comes from the study of US economic history. Claudia Goldin and Lawrence Katz tell the story of the United States' world-leading investments in education beginning early in the nineteenth century and persisting through the expansion of college opportunity in the 1960s.[4] The United States, for example, invested heavily in expanding high schools at a time when European countries thought that such further education should be restricted to a narrow elite. Katz and Goldin marry this story of expanding educational opportunity to the parallel story of the relentless advance of technology over the same period and show how technical advances increase the demand for education and the productivity of educated labor, resulting in a growing economy and a healthy economic return to educational investments. Katz and Goldin attribute the lagging performance of the US economy since the 1980s in large part to slowed expansion of educational attainment in the United States.

The persistent increase in demand for educated workers in the face of a slowdown in the growth of supply of educated workers has meant that the rate of return to education—particularly to higher education—has in recent years risen to levels much

---

[3] A valuable introduction to the voluminous literature on returns to education can be found in Dominic Brewer and Patrick McEwan, eds., *Economics of Education* (San Diego, CA: Elsevier Press, 2010).
[4] See Claudia Goldin and Lawrence F. Katz, *The Race between Education and Technology* (Cambridge, MA: Harvard University Press, 2008).

higher than ever before. Avery and Turner estimate that the economic return to a college degree tripled for women between 1965 and 2009 and rose nearly as fast for men.[5]

Of course, a high average return to investments in education does not mean that every person who goes to college will benefit. We know that gains are substantially greater for those who complete a degree or program than for those who drop out, and we know as well that many factors other than college attendance affect lifetime earnings. We also embrace the truth that the benefits of education extend well beyond those of a bigger paycheck or even a financially better-off society. Few Americans, however, have the luxury of divorcing their plans for education from their concern for a secure livelihood or for a more prosperous society.

It's important to be clear that, from the perspective of society as a whole, the cost of today's investments must be borne *now*, as they are made. In the classic metaphor, if we want more guns, we must have less butter—and there is no magical way to import guns or butter from the future to avoid present sacrifice. As a society we have to decide how much by way of present consumption goods we are willing to give up in order to have a better future—the same trade-off we struggle with when we decide to devote present resources to improving physical infrastructure or when a corporation decides to invest in developing new products with its earnings rather than paying a higher dividend.

When we adopt this basic investment perspective and look at the matter from a society-wide point of view, fundamental questions to consider include these: How much should we invest? In

---

[5] Christopher Avery and Sarah Turner, "Are Students Borrowing Too Much—or Not Enough?" *Journal of Economic Perspectives* 26, no. 1 (2012): p.165–92.

whom should we invest? How can we make these investments as cost-effective as possible? And finally, how should the cost or sacrifice these investments require be shared across society?

These are core questions that our society needs to address as we look to the future. Yet much public discourse seems almost designed to avoid addressing these questions directly and instead gets "lost in the weeds." Distractions abound. For example, we talk less about how much society should invest in post-secondary education than about how we should *finance* the investment. To be sure, the distributive questions about who will bear the costs and who will gain most from the benefits of the investment are important—as well as often divisive. Still, the question of the right level of total investment is ultimately more consequential, even as it is tied in subtle ways to the financing questions. But all too often these discussions create the impression that if we can just be clever enough in devising financing schemes, we can make the cost of the investment disappear. Not true!

Somebody has to bear these costs when they occur. Very few recent high school graduates have, on their own, the wherewithal to cover their own full-time college expenses, including living expenses (take these as a proxy for forgone earnings) while they are going to school.[6] Those who start or return to college later in life rarely have substantial assets of their own to

---

[6] The idea of paying for college by going to school part-time and working part-time doesn't really solve the problem. Pay from a part-time job is likely to start and stay low, while productivity as a student—and the likelihood of finishing the job— probably go down when you string out the effort over more years. Also, delaying entry to the labor market while earning a college degree costs years of increased earning power. "Self-financing" in this way has downsides reminiscent of those associated with saving up to buy a house with cash.

draw on when studying. Thus, most college costs have historically been borne by other people in two basic ways:

1. Older adults may make gifts to the younger generation by covering their tuition and living costs, thus lowering their own consumption levels (or reducing accumulated savings) in order to enable members of the younger generation to have better lives. Relatively well-off parents may do this for their own children, citizens may pay taxes that allow governments to do it through taxes and appropriations, and the philanthropically inclined may do it through gifts to colleges and universities.

2. Alternatively, older adults may pay students' tuition and living expenses in exchange for promises that the students will pay them back later, out of the presumably higher earnings that a college education will bring them. In that case, the older (lending) generation accepts a reduction in current consumption to produce an investment return but gets paid back later out of the returns the education has provided to the younger (borrowing) generation. We are familiar in the United States with students borrowing as individuals, either from the federal government or from banks; in some countries, the intergenerational transfer happens collectively, as through a "graduate tax," a surcharge imposed on college graduates to pay society back for the government-provided education they received earlier. (In several US states, governors have floated this idea under the banner of "Pay It Forward.")[7]

---

[7] As of August 7, 2014, some version of "pay it forward" legislation had been introduced in twenty-two states, but it has so far not been enacted into law anywhere. Note that the generation voting on such legislation gets a benefit later generations

These two options, and combinations of them, are the *only* options for paying for college as long as the expenses of college (including the costs of living) exceed the amount that students can pay out of their own earnings while devoting the bulk of their time to learning. Either the present adult generation picks up the tab for the next generation's education (as well-off parents commonly do for their children) or the present adult generation loans students the money to pay for their education in exchange for the students' promise to pay the money back. In an ongoing society where the bulk of people go to college, these two systems actually look broadly similar in many ways—fifty-year-olds are either paying their parents' generation back for the education they received or they are paying their own children forward by covering the costs of their college education. Either way, it's people in their peak earning years who pay the cost of college. Of course the details matter, mostly in terms of how the benefits and costs are distributed across the population and in terms of who gets to go to college. But no matter how much we struggle over financing mechanisms, they won't help us answer the question of how much of an investment in education we as a society should make; nor will they ever eradicate the reality that investing in education requires sacrifice.

Sacrifice to what end? We must keep a strong focus on the fact that the purpose of education beyond high school is to equip people to lead more productive and rewarding lives. It is what students accomplish in college that matters. It is the knowledge and skills they gain that contribute lasting value to their lives. We are economists, but we certainly do not believe that earnings

---

miss out on. Members of the first generation already have their education and so don't have a graduate tax imposed. It's the students in school when the legislation passes that are the first who have to pay back for their education.

are the only measure of education's value, or that they are always the most important. There is good evidence that people emerge from college more civic-minded, more adept at parenting, and more likely to manage their health ably than others are.[8] Still, earnings really do matter, and one thing students (not to mention parents) expect from college, and should expect, is that it will help them build successful careers.[9] This is especially important for first-generation and disadvantaged students.

The earnings evidence tells us unequivocally that what matters for students' lives is not starting college but finishing successfully—completing a degree or certificate. It is what students accomplish in college—the skills they master and the knowledge they acquire—that justifies both the social and the private investment that college demands. Just getting in the door or even sticking around for a year or two adds much less value.

We worry that the great emphasis on access and affordability in current public policy discussions may drown out the need for a strong focus on the effectiveness of colleges in educating the students who enroll. We find it unsettling that there are four-year colleges in this country that continue to be accredited and receive public financial support where as few as 10 or 15 percent of their students complete degrees. It is particularly demoralizing to realize that many students leave these colleges not only with no degree but also with significant debt. As we explain later, these are the students who are most likely to default on

[8] Sandy Baum and Kathleen Payea, *Education Pays: The Benefits of Higher Education for Individuals and Society* (New York: College Board, 2004), available at www.college board.com/prod_downloads/press/cost04/EducationPays2004.pdf.

[9] Growing availability of earnings data has led some analysts and observers to slide from the reasonable wish that a bachelor's degree should provide access to good jobs to the foolish and destructive idea that students should choose colleges and majors with the aim of maximizing their post-college earnings.

their loans. However, the first order of business is not to make these places cheaper so students can drop out debt free but instead to make them substantially more effective in producing satisfied graduates.

In our view, the leading question about college finance is not how to make college appear to be free but how to share the costs equitably and aim the resources where they are most needed. The leading question about college enrollment is less about getting people to start college and more about getting a broader range of Americans to succeed in obtaining an education that will serve them well for many years to come.

PART II

Pressing National Needs

Achieving Higher Levels of Educational Attainment

Inadequate as they may be (and are) in providing anything like a full picture of the achievements of an educational system, educational attainment rates, expressed as the percentage of a specified age group that earned a given educational credential, are a useful starting point in judging how we are doing in creating the human capital that every country needs.

OECD Comparisons

The broadest perspective is provided by international comparisons. The OECD continues to do a conscientious job of summarizing and comparing more or less comparable data on educational attainment across the thirty-four OECD members and ten other countries. The OECD provides this succinct summary of why educational attainment matters in all countries:

> Higher levels of educational attainment are associated with several positive individual and social outcomes. Data in previous editions of *Education at a Glance* [the annual OECD

publication] have shown that individuals with high educational attainment generally have better health, are more socially engaged, have higher employment rates and have higher relative earnings. Higher proficiency on skills such as literacy and numeracy is also strongly associated with higher levels of formal education.[1]

The most recent OECD data are for 2014, and the OECD sorts their information on postsecondary (or "tertiary") educational attainment into categories that correspond roughly to the American categories of pre-baccalaureate credentials (including associate degrees), bachelors' degrees, masters' degrees, and PhDs and equivalent. We will focus here primarily on the broadest category that sums over all these levels of attainment, although examining the more detailed categories would not change the basic story.

If we look first at this broad category, encompassing associate and higher degrees, for the entire population ages 25 to 64, the results are consistent with the popular sense that the United States still stands at or near the top of the world-league tables: the tertiary attainment rate in the US for the entire 25–64 group was 45 percent in 2014, compared with an average for all OECD countries of 36 percent—a nine point advantage. Only two countries, Canada and Japan, had higher tertiary attainment rates (55 and 49 percent, respectively.)

The same story holds true if we focus in on the attainment of BAs or higher degrees in the 25 to 64 year old population. The United States again easily exceeds the OECD average (34 per-

[1] Organisation for Economic Co-operation and Development (OECD), *Education at a Glance Interim Report (Paris,* January 2015), p. 9.

cent versus 28 percent) and only Luxembourg (35 percent) has a higher attainment rate than the United States.

On a much less positive note for those of us in the United States, the OECD findings are much less encouraging—indeed, downright discouraging—*when we look at trends.* An easy way to gain a sense of what is happening is by looking at the "all-tertiary" results in 2014 for a younger age group (25 to 34 year olds). While the US still beats the OECD average in attainment rates, the gap is now much narrower, 46 percent versus 41 percent. And there are now seven countries with rates higher than the US rate: Australia, Canada, Ireland, Korea, Luxembourg, and the United Kingdom. This same pattern of narrowing in differences is apparent within the narrower group of 25 to 34 year olds with BAs or higher degrees. While it is certainly true that the precise definitions of these classifications vary across countries, there is no denying that the United States has lost considerable ground, and lost ground rather rapidly.

OECD data that compare tertiary attainment rates for 25 to 34 year olds for 2000 with those for 2014 make this point particularly well.[2] On average over that period, tertiary attainment for 25 to 34 year olds rose from 26 percent to 41 percent, a 15 point gain. The greatest gain was for Korea, which rose from an already high 37 percent in 2000 to a remarkable 68 percent in 2014—a 31 percentage point gain. Over that same period, US attainment among 25 to 34 year olds grew by only eight percentage points, from 38 percent to 46 percent. Only three countries from among the 28 for which data are available had lower

[2] OECD, *Education at a Glance 2015*, Table A14a.

attainment growth in percentage terms (Finland, Germany, and Spain) while two other countries (Mexico and Belgium) matched the US's slow growth.

The United States has clearly lost the major advantage it once enjoyed in providing post-secondary education to a large share of its population—an ominous finding in an increasingly knowledge-driven world.[3] This is not a question of "beating the opposition"—we all benefit when the world's countries make smart investments in their people. Rather, we hope that the US can learn from the examples of other countries. To be sure, the United States continues to enjoy an outstanding reputation for providing graduate education at the highest level and for generating impressive research results across a broad array of fields of knowledge. Both international rankings and evidence from student choices (with large numbers of foreign students eager to pursue graduate work in this country) speak to the accomplishments of US universities at the highest levels of achievement. But the high standing of leading US research universities, judged by the quality of their doctoral and research programs, should not blind us to the fact that we are rapidly losing the advantage we once enjoyed in overall levels of educational attainment—if we have not already lost it.

[3] David Autor, in a widely acclaimed article ("Skills, Education, and the Rise of Earnings Inequality among the 'Other 99 Percent,'" *Science*, May 2014), puts the fundamental proposition this way: "A technologically advanced economy requires a literate, numerate, and technically and scientifically trained workforce to develop ideas, manage complex organizations, deliver healthcare services, provide financing and insurance, administer government services, and operate critical infrastructure" (p. 845). Autor goes on to argue that "the ongoing process of machine substitution for routine human labor complements advanced workers who excel in abstract tasks that harness problem-solving ability, intuition, creativeness and persuasion—tasks that are at present difficult to automate but essential to perform" (p. 846).

US Data in More Detail

Within the United States, President Obama has recognized clearly that we need to dramatically increase our educational attainment rate. In his first address to a joint session of Congress, the president set a "bold, if daunting, goal to lead the world in [educational attainment] by 2020."[4] The Lumina Foundation and its president, Jamie P. Merisotis, continue to emphasize the importance of this goal, to present state-by-state data on progress to date, and to urge everyone on. In his 2014 report, Merisotis strikes an optimistic note, calling attention both to survey data showing that "the hunger for higher education is stronger than ever" and to a recent uptick in the educational attainment rate.[5]

To seek precise measures of "educational attainment rates" (which are very different from "college completion rates"[6]) is to pursue something akin to a "will-o-the-wisp." Sandy Baum and her collaborators Alisa Federico Cunningham and Courtney Tanenbaum have produced a most useful report that explains in great detail how hard it is to combine sources of data and why different sources produce different answers to what may seem like the same question.[7] This report is concerned primarily

[4] Kelly Field, "6 Years in and 6 to Go, Only Modest Progress on Obama's College-Completion Goal," *Chronicle of Higher Education*, January 20, 2015. This article contains a lengthy discussion of the origins of the goal, the difficulty of attaining it, and its importance.

[5] Lumina Foundation, *A Stronger Nation through Higher Education*, 2014 edition (Indianapolis).

[6] College completion rates measure the percentage of those who start college who finish, as contrasted with educational attainment rates, which measure the percentage of a given population group that eventually attains a credential of one kind or another.

[7] Sandy Baum, Alisa Federico Cunningham, and Courtney Tanenbaum, "Educational Attainment: Understanding the Data," working paper, Graduate School of Education and Human Development, George Washington University, Washington,

with circumstances today, whereas we are at least as interested in trends as in current conditions—even as we recognize the pitfalls involved in trying to construct a reliable time series. Complications notwithstanding, it is possible to gain a reasonably clear sense of "the big picture"—where we have been and where we are headed, as well as where we are today. We are indebted to Matthew Staiger for carefully constructing a time series from 1968 through 2013 for the educational attainment of 25- to 29-year-olds in the United States (a leading indicator) using data from the Current Population Survey (CPS), and to Lisa Krueger for updating this work to include 2014.

Figure 1 indicates that the percentage of the 25- to 29-year-old population holding BAs or higher degrees increased from 30 percent in 2007 to 34 percent in 2014.[8] We also see that if one combines holders of BAs with holders of associate degrees, the pattern is essentially the same. The data reported in the Lumina Foundation report show the same modest uptick in educational attainment over the past few years. This is most welcome news given the fact that, following a long period of steady increases in educational attainment dating back to the "high school movement" of the early 1900s, our country seemed to be stuck on a no-increase plateau from about 1975 to the early 1990s.[9]

DC, April 2015, available at http://gsehd.gwu.edu/sites/default/files/documents/Educational_Attainment_FINAL_Report_4.27.pdf.

[8] This figure (originally with data through 2013) was incorporated into a paper presented by Bowen at the DeLange Conference at Rice University, "Technology: Its Potential Impact on the National Need to Improve Educational Outcomes and Control Costs," October 13, 2014, available at www.sr.ithaka.org/publications/technology-its-potential-impact-on-the-national-need-to-improve-educational-outcomes-and-control-costs/.

[9] For an extended discussion of trends, see William G. Bowen, Matthew M. Chingos, and Michael S. McPherson, *Crossing the Finish Line: Completing College at America's Public Universities* (Princeton, NJ: Princeton University Press, 2009), and

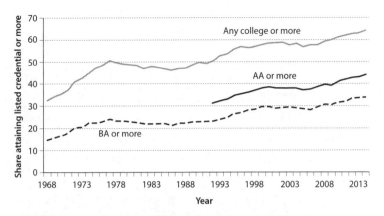

FIGURE 1: Educational Attainment of 25- to 29-year-olds, 1968–2014
Source: US Census Bureau and Bureau of Labor Statistics, *Current Population Survey* (Washington, DC: 2015), available at www.census.gov.cps.

However, there are two reasons that we should be very careful not to assume that this uptick necessarily represents the beginning of a new stage of continuing increases in educational attainment. First, as the Lumina Foundation report recognizes, changing demographics in America warn us that population groups with below-average attainment rates (especially Hispanics) are growing relative to the main group with above-average attainment rates (the white population); indeed, Lumina calculates that if attainment rates were to stay the same for all racial or ethnic subgroups, the overall attainment rate would fall by roughly 1 percentage point between now and 2025.[10] Another demographic aspect of recent trends is that it is women, not men, who have been enrolling and graduating in larger

the pioneering work on this subject by Goldin and Katz in *The Race between Education and Technology*.
[10] *A Stronger Nation through Higher Education*, 2014 edition, p. 2.

numbers.[11] It is unclear what this (not well understood) trend implies about the future path of overall attainment rates.

The second reason not to exaggerate the long-term importance of the uptick is that it is hard to know how much of it is due to the 2007–08 recession and the subsequent recovery. As is well known, recessions induce more students to enroll in college and eventually to graduate for the simple reason that the main alternative—entering the labor market—is less attractive when jobs are hard to find. Thus, it is not surprising that full-time undergraduate enrollment was 9.5 percent lower in 2015 than in 2011 after increasing by 21 percent from 2005 to 2010. The recent decline has been driven primarily by a drop in enrollment in four-year for-profit institutions (down 22.8 percent) and in two-year institutions (down 16.4 percent). If we focus on four-year not-for-profit institutions, including both public and private non-profits, enrollment declined much more modestly (by 2.6 percent from 2011 to 2015); but it still declined.[12]

In short, we simply do not know how much of the recent uptick in age-specific attainment rates is cyclical (due to the recession and the recovery from it) and how much is struc-

---

[11] National Center for Education Statistics (NCES), *The Condition of Education 2012*, NCES 2012–045 (Washington, DC), indicator 47.

[12] According to a May 2015 report issued by the National Student Clearinghouse, "total college enrollment fell again this year, driven primarily by the departure of older students finding employment in an improving economy" (Andy Thomason, "Even Private Colleges Feel the Pain as Enrollment Falls Again," *Chronicle of Higher Education*, May 14, 2015). See also *National Student Clearinghouse Student Research Center Term Enrollment Estimates*, Spring 2005–Spring 2015, available at http://nscresearchcenter.org. The report also states that "enrollment at private four-year colleges dropped for the first time in several years," and that "institutions enrolling fewer than 3,000 students saw a bigger drop, of 2.4 percent"—a finding relevant to the debate over the closing of Sweet Briar College. Apparently, enrollment at community colleges dropped significantly at the same time that enrollment at public four-year institutions stayed steady.

tural.[13] It is clear that some states and some institutions are putting increasing emphasis on raising these rates, and we can only hope that such efforts prove to have lasting effects.

Even more fundamentally, one can question whether even the current level of attainment represents significant cognitive accomplishments by many students—as Arum and Roksa do in their widely cited book *Academically Adrift: Limited Learning on College Campuses*.[14] However, this is an instance in which such a negative perception is clearly overdone. The most widely reported claim made by Arum and Roska—that 45 percent of students made "no measurable gains in general skills"—is simply wrong. As both Alexander Astin and John Etchemendy have explained at length, this erroneous claim is due to a common statistical fallacy—namely, a failure to distinguish false positives from false negatives. The fact that 45 percent of students failed to pass a statistical threshold designed to assure us that they in fact improved their basic skills means only that we don't know how many of these students did in fact improve their basic skills—conceivably quite a large number.[15] Overall, these flawed findings could well be interpreted as encouraging rather than discouraging.

Broad-gauged assaults on the content of education today have become increasingly common. There are, fortunately, a

---

[13] See Sarah E. Turner, "The Impact of the Financial Crisis on Faculty Labor Markets," and Bridget Terry Long, "The Financial Crisis and College Enrollment: How Have Students and Their Families Responded?," in *How the Financial Crisis and Great Recession Affected Higher Education*, edited by Jeffrey R. Brown and Caroline M. Hoxby (Chicago: University of Chicago Press, 2015).

[14] Richard Arum and Josipa Roksa, *Academically Adrift: Limited Learning on College Campuses* (Chicago: University of Chicago Press, 2011).

[15] See Alexander Astin, "The Promise and Peril of Outcomes Assessment," *Chronicle of Higher Education*, September 3, 2013. See also John Etchemendy "Are Our Colleges and Universities Failing Us?" *Carnegie Reporter* 7, no. 3 (Winter 2014).

number of eloquent defenses of liberal education as not only life-enriching but also valuable from a vocational standpoint at a time when success so often depends on flexibility, creativity, and the ability to think across boundaries of all kinds. Fareed Zakaria in the *Washington Post* states: "Critical thinking is, in the end, the only way to protect American jobs."[16] David Autor, the MIT economist who has carefully studied the impact of technology and globalization on labor, writes that "human tasks that have proved most amenable to computerization are those that follow explicit, codifiable procedures—such as multiplication—where computers now vastly exceed human labor in speed, quality, accuracy, and cost efficiency. Tasks that have proved most vexing to automate are those that demand flexibility, judgment, and common sense—skills that we understand only tacitly—for example, developing a hypothesis or organizing a closet."[17] Still, critics abound, and that is fine—indeed healthy. But some are more thoughtful than others. Brian Rosenberg has written a characteristically wise (and, to our way of thinking, devastating) review of William Deresiewicz's facile assessments of the state of higher education.[18]

Our worries about the content and ambition of today's post-secondary education focus, if anything, in the other direction. Many two-year colleges, as well as some four-year colleges, place so much emphasis on short-term vocational preparation (like learning in detail how to operate a particular machine) that the

[16] See Fareed Zakaria, "Why America's Obsession with STEM Education Is Dangerous," *Washington Post*, March 26, 2015.

[17] See David Autor, "Polanyi's Paradox and the Shape of Employment Growth," draft prepared for the Federal Bank of Kansas City's economic policy symposium Re-evaluating Labor Market Dynamics, August 21–23, 2014, in Jackson Hole, Wyoming, available at http://economics.mit.edu/files/9835.

[18] See Brian Rosenberg, "My William Deresiewicz Problem," *Chronicle of Higher Education*, September 2, 2015.

capacities Autor and Zakaria speak of—critical thinking, judgment, the exercise of common sense—may be neglected, producing an education that will very quickly become obsolete. It's not uncommon to find that graduates of some two-year vocational programs earn more than typical BA graduates do in their first year in the labor market. But it is quite clear that the earning difference switches decisively over time to favor those who have the wider-ranging experience of bachelor's-level education; the "option value" of the BA degree in permitting access to advanced degrees is an important part of this equation.

The main conclusion to be drawn from this examination of attainment rates in the United States is that they are simply too low to ensure the success of this country in a rapidly evolving global economy, and too low to give many Americans the improved life chances that they deserve.

Raising College Completion Rates in the United States

Attainment rates are of course the product of two factors: enrollment in higher education and the fraction of those students who enroll who complete their studies. It is often difficult to disentangle these two factors, and studies of low attainment (achievement) rates do not always parse them out. For example, David Autor focuses simply on skill premiums. In his widely quoted article in *Science*, Autor demonstrates that the skill premium associated with cognitive achievement is much higher in the United States than in any of the other twenty-one developed countries for which data are available.[19] This is a strong market signal that more Americans need to gain these skills—primarily

---

[19] Autor, "Skills, Education, and the Rise of Earnings Inequality."

by enrolling in post-secondary programs and then completing their studies—but other avenues to skill attainment are also relevant.

We know that degree completion per se (as compared with simply completing an equivalent number of years of college) is strongly associated with distinctly above-average employment outcomes.[20] This is an important reason why, in this section of our book, we concentrate on completion rates. As we stressed in the prologue, it is clearly not good enough simply to increase the number of people who start out. "Crossing the finish line" matters greatly. There are, we suspect, two reasons for this. First, completing degree programs presumably means that the student has mastered some organized structure of content rather than simply having completed what could have been a smorgasbord of individual courses. Second, students who complete degree programs have demonstrated a capacity to "get it done"— and the personal qualities involved, including perseverance, are highly likely to contribute to success in job markets and other facets of life.[21]

All types of institutions experienced moderate gains in the six-year completion rate for 2006 to 2008 entrants, with the striking exception of four-year for-profit institutions. The public four-year rate went from 60.6 to 62.9 percent, the private four-year rate from 71.5 to 73.6 percent, and the public two-year rate from 36.3 to 39.1 percent. But the six-year completion

---

[20] See Bowen, Chingos, and McPherson, *Crossing the Finish Line*, especially p. 9.

[21] It's hard to know to what extent students learn in college to be more persevering or whether those who succeed had acquired the disposition to do so earlier. Our unscientific impression, based on introspection and decades of teaching, is that the experience of successfully completing long-term projects is self-reinforcing. If that is right, helping more people to complete college is even more important than would otherwise be the case.

rates at for-profit four-year institutions fell from 42.3 percent to 38.9 percent—enough to fully offset the gains in the other institutional categories.

The most recent data available on six-year completion rates from the National Student Clearinghouse (rates that take account of transfers and thus show how many students complete degrees at any college, not just at the college first attended) are for the cohort that entered college in 2009. As of the spring of 2015, the six-year completion rate for first-time, degree-seeking students in US colleges and universities who began post-secondary education in the fall of 2008 was 52.9 percent. This rate is down 2.1 percent from the comparable rate the previous year, and the National Student Clearing House says that this decline was "across the board." It no doubt reflects the improving job market and is a good reminder of the need to take job market conditions into account in interpreting completion rate data.[22]

Having written an entire book on completion rates at America's public universities (and, in the process, having built a huge database of student outcomes at these universities),[23] we are going to be economical here in commenting on "the big picture." These points deserve to be highlighted.

First, there is no question that the limited success of American higher education in meeting the national need for higher completion rates is due in no small measure to the large number of students who begin a program of higher education and then end up dropping out. A recent expansion of the data available on student debt and repayment patterns underscores the severe

[22] See Paul Fain, "College Completion Rates Decline More Rapidly," *Inside Higher Ed*, November 17, 2015, available at www.insidehighered.com/quicktakes/2015/11/17/college-completion-rates-decline-more-rapidly.

[23] See Bowen, Chingos, and McPherson, *Crossing the Finish Line*.

consequences of dropping out of college. The highest default rates are found among students who have borrowed relatively little, often less than $10,000, to attend programs they don't complete. Meanwhile, students who borrow more substantial sums in the course of completing bachelor's programs (more than $25,000 on average among those who borrow) have much lower default rates.[24]

Of course, some amount of attrition is to be expected in any system, because some students who have started out learn that higher education is not for them. But certainly many students drop out because of obstacles that could be overcome. Money is an important issue in an era when cutbacks in state support have driven up prices and need-based aid hasn't always kept up. Students and families too often face difficult decisions about where to go to college and how to pay for it in an excessively complicated system that simply has failed to pay sufficient attention to the need for high-quality academic and financial guidance for students and families—especially for first-generation college students. Indeed, on the financial side, while some students may borrow too much—or from the wrong sources— others, trying to avoid debt at all costs, may take on heroic work schedules that are not compatible with completing degree programs in a timely way. As bad as college counseling often is in high schools that serve disadvantaged students, the situation is even worse for older adults, such as those returning from the armed services, whose main source of "guidance" may be ads on a bus or a marketer at a for-profit college.

---

[24] Susan Dynarski, "Why Students with the Smallest Debts Have the Larger Problem," *New York Times*, August 31, 2015; US Department of Education (USED), *College Scorecard*, https://collegescorecard.ed.gov/data/.

A sensitive but important contributor to low success rates in achieving bachelor's degree completion is decisions by students to start at community colleges rather than at four-year institutions. The research results are crystal clear: students who begin at four-year colleges have a *much* higher probability of receiving a BA degree than do students who aspire to earn BAs but who start out at two-year institutions, a result that holds after controlling for differences in pre-college levels of academic preparation. Differences in BA completion rates between the two groups are much higher than one might have expected them to be—on the order of 30 percentage points, or even more. Another surprise is that these differences are just as prevalent among students with modest academic credentials as they are among students with higher SAT scores and better grades in secondary school. We might expect that the least well-prepared students would be more frustrated (intimidated?) than other students starting at four-year institutions and that students with less strong academic credentials might be better off getting acclimated to higher education at a two-year college. Using an exceptionally rich set of data from North Carolina, we learned that this expectation was simply not true for students in that state.[25]

More recently, a large-scale study of students in Florida using a regression discontinuity design has demonstrated that academically marginal students with grades just above the threshold for admissions eligibility at a large public university (Florida International University) are much more likely than students

---

[25] Bowen, Chingos, and McPherson, *Crossing the Finish Line*, especially pp. 134–40. Our co-author, Matthew M. Chingos, deserves the credit for devising a series of tests using controls of various kinds, including propensity measures, to examine the effects of starting at two-year versus four-year institutions.

just below the threshold to attend any university. These "above-threshold" students go on to enjoy substantial earnings gains over the "just-below-threshold" students, and these gains are largest for male students and poor students. The important conclusion is that it is not just well-prepared students who benefit from attending mid-level four-year institutions.[26]

From a policy standpoint, this research warns that President Obama's proposal to make community college free for a large portion of the student population carries significant risk. To be sure, lowering the price of community college may improve the chances that students who would not otherwise have attended any college will go somewhere. We also have to recognize, however, that by changing the relative price of education in the two- and four-year sectors, the Obama proposal may actually lower degree completion rates for students induced to choose a community college option over the chance to enroll from the start at a four-year institution.[27]

The broader question is to what extent completion rates are lowered by failures of students to attend academically strong institutions for which they are qualified. By now there is a considerable literature documenting the importance of an appropriate "match" in determining educational outcomes. In brief, these studies show that students who enroll at institutions with test scores (and other academic credentials) at or above their own levels do much better in earning degrees, and in earning them

[26] Seth D. Zimmerman, "The Returns to College Admission for Academically Marginal Students," *Journal of Labor Economics*, October 2014, pp. 711–54.

[27] Bowen, Chingos, and McPherson, in *Crossing the Finish Line*, discuss the sometimes perverse effects of programs designed to increase community college enrollment in various states, including the New Jersey STARS (Student Tuition Assistance Reward Scholarship) program (pp. 134–35).

in a timely way, than do students who "undermatch"—by which we mean simply that they go to schools that are less selective than schools for which their qualifications could well have led to their admission.

The early study of race-sensitive admissions by Bowen and Bok made some contribution to this discussion by studying rigorously the "fit" hypothesis, which was used by opponents of affirmative action to argue that disappointing academic results for minority students were due in some (many?) instances to the fact that these students were recruited by institutions that were academically stronger than they were, with the alleged result that these minority students were intimidated and simply could not compete with their better-credentialed classmates. Using the College and Beyond database, Bowen and Bok demonstrated that this "fit" hypothesis is simply wrong. In fact, minority students with "below-average" credentials did *much* better at the highly selective schools in the database that admitted them than did those with similar credentials who attended less selective schools.[28]

The Chicago Consortium has played a pioneering role in introducing this basic notion of "match" into the study of why large numbers of well-prepared high school students of all races fail to complete college. The reports of the Chicago Consortium in 2008 and 2009 documented the surprising extent to which students who had worked hard and earned good grades in the

[28] William G. Bowen and Derek Bok, *The Shape of the River: Long-Term Consequences of Considering Race in College and University Admissions* (Princeton, NJ: Princeton University Press, 1998), pp. 59–68. This study discusses the variety of reasons for this outcome, which has been replicated by other data, including those for black men attending a wide range of public universities (Bowen, Chingos, and McPherson, *Crossing the Finish Line*, pp. 208–11).

Chicago public schools attended colleges that were less selective than the schools for which these students were presumptively qualified—and then, in many cases, did not graduate.[29] In *Crossing the Finish Line*, Bowen, Chingos, and McPherson augmented these results by using the rich set of data from North Carolina we referred to earlier. They found both substantial "undermatching" among North Carolina students of many kinds (especially, but by no means only, minority students) and substantial penalties for undermatching in terms of both four-year and six-year graduation rates.[30]

Subsequently, Hoxby and Turner have contributed to this literature by demonstrating that simply providing more information about college choices to well-prepared high school students improves "matches."[31] And the Zimmerman study cited earlier complements the work of Hoxby and Turner by demonstrating that attending a mid-level public university rather than a community college or no college at all is important for lower-achieving students as well as those who are exceptionally well prepared. Evidence rebutting the mismatch hypothesis continues to accumulate. Alon, in a study that compares experiences in the United States and Israel, finds absolutely no sup-

---

[29] See Melissa Roderick, Jenny Nagaoka, Vanessa Coca, Eliza Moeller, Karen Roddie, Jamiliyah Gilliam, and Desmond Patton, "From High School to the Future: Potholes on the Road to College," Consortium on Chicago School Research, March 2008, and Melissa Roderick, Jenny Nagaoka, Vanessa Coca, and Eliza Moeller, "From High to the Future: Making Hard Work Pay Off," Consortium on Chicago School Research, April 2009.

[30] Bowen, Chingos, and McPherson, *Crossing the Finish Line*, pp. 102–11.

[31] See Caroline M. Hoxby and Sarah E. Turner, "Expanding College Opportunity for High-Achieving, Low-Income Students," Stanford Institute for Economic Policy Research, 2013, available at http://siepr.stanford.edu.

port for mismatch claims in any of the voluminous data that she examines.[32]

More generally, there is strong evidence that the selectivity of the institution attended, public or private, has a pronounced effect on completion rates. Otherwise comparable students (based on "observables," such as scores, grades, race or ethnicity, and family background) who go to relatively selective schools graduate at appreciably higher rates than their counterparts who go to less selective institutions. We suspect that this powerfully persistent pattern is due to some combination of peer effects, ingrained expectations at the selective institutions (that, for example, everyone will graduate in four years), and unusually rich teaching resources.[33]

While guiding students toward colleges where they have the best chance of succeeding is important, so is improving the performance of institutions that students at high risk of dropping out are, de facto, most likely to attend. The instructional challenges

---

[32] See Sigal Alon, *Race, Class and Affirmative Action* (New York, Russell Sage Foundation, 2015. See also the comprehensive blogpost by Matthew M. Chingos that surveys recent studies and critiques the methodology of some, "Affirmative action 'mismatch' theory isn't supported by credible evidence," Urban Institute, *Urban Wire*, December 10, 2015, available at http://www.urban.org/urban-wire/affirmative -action-mismatch-theory-isnt-supported-credible-evidence.

[33] Bowen, Chingos, and McPherson, *Crossing the Finish Line*, chapter 10. The reluctance of some to acknowledge these factors (and these findings) is puzzling. At a memorable meeting in Washington, DC, called to discuss *The Shape of the River*, Bowen recalls that a white woman challenged the importance of encouraging minority students to go to selective institutions, asserting that there are many other fine institutions that they could attend (as surely there are). An African American woman responded as follows: "Are you telling me that all these white folks beating down the doors to get in Stanford are just stupid? Or are you telling me that it matters for your children to go to Stanford, but it shouldn't matter for mine?" Silence followed.

for these "broad-access" institutions are surely greater than those faced by institutions that are in a position to handpick their students, yet they are generally expected to get by with lower levels of per-student support than their more selective peers. Attendance at poorly resourced institutions also helps explain increased time-to-degree.

One fact of over-riding importance is that the likelihood of completing a degree depends heavily on a student's success in passing "foundational" courses in subjects such as mathematics. About two-thirds of all students who enter two-year institutions enroll in at least one remedial course within six years of entry.[34] A study by the Community College Research Center (CCRC) at Columbia University found that more than 59 percent of entering students are placed in a developmental mathematics course and 33 percent are placed in developmental reading.[35] The same study found that 80 percent of all students who are placed into developmental mathematics fail to successfully complete any college-level math course within three years of entry. According to Anthony S. Bryk, president of the Carnegie Foundation for the Advancement of Teaching: "If you do not get out of developmental mathematics, you cannot acquire credits to transfer to a four-year institution, and you often cannot get access to vocational and technical training programs. The bumper sticker for this problem is 'Developmental mathematics is where aspira-

[34] Based on data from the NCES Beginning Postsecondary Student Longitudinal Survey, 2009.
[35] Based on data from a Community College Research Center (CCRC) study of over 250,000 students at fifty-seven community colleges in the Achieving the Dream initiative. See Thomas Bailey, Dong Wok Jeong, and Sun-Woo Cho, "Student Progression through Developmental Sequences in Community Colleges," *CCRC Brief* 45 (September 2010).

tions go to die.'"[36] We return to the question of the potential of adaptive learning pedagogies to address this problem in part III.

Reducing Time-to-Degree

If disappointingly low completion rates are one major problem facing higher education (as they are!), long time-to-degree is certainly another. Unfortunately, it is hard to interpret aggregative time-series data from the CPS that one might have hoped could document the seriousness of this problem. These data show that in the early post–World War II years, roughly 60 percent of BA recipients received their degree by age 22, whereas more recently, this percentage has hovered around 40 percent.[37] However, it would be wrong to assign full responsibility for this trend to longer time-to-degree because we know that the fraction of students beginning college later in life has also increased markedly over this period.

Whatever the time path has been, long time-to-degree is a problem at the major public universities we studied in *Crossing the Finish Line*. We also know that the tendency to take more time to graduate than the (old-fashioned?) norm of four years is not due to students' accumulating more credits (learning

---

[36] See Gay M. Clyburn, "Improving on the American Dream: Mathematics Pathways to Student Success," *Change: The Magazine of Higher Learning*," September–October 2013, available at www.changemag.org/Archives/Back%20Issues/2013/September -October%202013/american-dream-full.html.

[37] We are indebted to Matthew Staiger for updating the CPS data compiled for birth cohorts from 1945 through 1970 by Sarah E. Turner in "Going to College and Finishing College," in *College Choices: The Economics of Where to Go, and How to Pay For It*, edited by Caroline M. Hoxby (Cambridge, MA: National Bureau of Economic Research, September 2004), figure 1.6.

more).[38] Rather, it is due to some mix of other factors—changing enrollment patterns, students' failing and repeating courses, stopping out, and so on. The consequence, of course, is higher costs per degree for both students and institutions—higher outlays that are basically unproductive. Longer time-to-degree also encourages (requires?) students to borrow more, and in some cases to borrow more money than they can repay out of their future earnings—especially if they end up failing to graduate.

A valuable window on the nature and extent of this problem is provided by a careful comparison of evidence by Bound, Lovenheim, and Turner from two National Education Longitudinal Study databases (NELS-72 and NELS-88).[39] As the authors explain, these micro-level longitudinal databases have important advantages over the aggregative CPS data: "The [micro] data include measures of pre-collegiate achievement.... [Also,] these data identify the colleges attended by students, permitting us to analyze outcomes for different sets of collegiate institutions." This analysis yields three major findings:

1. The authors find "no evidence that changing student preparedness for college or student demographic characteristics can explain any of the time to degree increases [evident in these data]. Indeed, the observable characteristics of college graduates, including high school test scores,

---

[38] Bowen, Chingos, and McPherson, *Crossing the Finish Line*, pp. 66–67. Matthew Chingos deserves the credit for having parsed out this important distinction.

[39] John Bound, Michael F. Lovenheim, and Sarah Turner, "Increasing Time to Baccalaureate Degree in the United States," Population Studies Center Research Report 10–698, University of Michigan, Ann Arbor, April 2010, published later in various places and as NBER Working Paper 15892 in April 2010. This is by far the best analysis we have found, and, to the best of our knowledge, there is no subsequent work that challenges any of the findings in this study.

have become more favorable in terms of predicted time to degree across cohorts."[40]

2. "In contrast," they continue, "we find evidence that decreases in institutional resources at [many] public colleges and universities are important for explaining changes in time to degree.... The declines in resources per student at public sector colleges and universities predict some of the observed extension of time to degree."[41] The increased stratification of American higher education has been an important factor. Longer time-to-degree is concentrated among students at less selective public institutions, and the mix of enrollment has shifted toward these resource-poor institutions.[42]

3. The authors also report: "The dramatic rise in student employment and the comparatively large increases in time to degree among students from lower-income families are suggestive of a relationship between increased difficulties students have in financing college and increasing time to degree."[43] As we will discuss in more detail later, students

---

[40] Bound, Lovenheim, and Turner, "Increasing Time to Baccalaureate Degree," p. 2.

[41] Ibid.

[42] Ibid., table 1. In fact, time-to-degree *decreased* at the highly selective private institutions. As Bound, Lovenheim, and Turner explain, top-tier private and public institutions make few adjustments in enrollment in response to increasing demand, whereas enrollment is relatively elastic among public universities outside the most selective few. And at these institutions, "We expect increased demand to lead to reductions in resources per student because the increased enrollment is not met with a commensurate increase in appropriations from public sources and other non-tuition revenues" (p. 9).

[43] Bound, Lovenheim, and Turner, "Increasing Time to Baccalaureate Degree," p. 2. See also Cathy Sandeen's article on problems facing small colleges (such as Sweet Briar), where she emphasizes both affordability issues and long time-to-degree ("Here's What I Learned from the Near-Death of a Small College," *Time*, July 3, 2015).

who feel compelled to work longer hours while in school (because of higher net tuition costs) appear to pay a large penalty in terms of prolonged time-to-degree.

These sources of the problem of longer time-to-degree are hardly trivial. But they do offer some opportunities for improvement, as we will argue in the next part of this study. Tempting as it is to place the lion's share of the blame for greater time-to-degree on the secondary schools and/or on demographic trends, the data refute such explanations.

In sum, it is highly likely that the prospect of long time-to-degree deters some students from ever starting—never mind finishing—their degree programs, and thus contributes directly to low overall levels of educational attainment. Prolonged time-to-degree, then, is wasteful in and of itself, as well as a deterrent to raising completion and attainment rates, and, as we will see in the next section, a contributor to increasing disparities in educational outcomes related to a child's place in the socioeconomic hierarchy. It is also related to the widely discussed (and often exaggerated) upward trend in student borrowing, which we discuss under "Achieving Affordability."

Reducing Disparities in Outcomes by Socioeconomic Status and Race or Ethnicity

Most of us brought up since World War II have been taught to believe that higher education in America is an "engine of opportunity" rather than a "bastion of privilege."[44] That is certainly

---

[44] See Andrew Delbanco, "Our Universities: The Outrageous Reality," *New York Review of Books*, July 9, 2015, for interesting early references to assertions that higher education could be the great equalizer. For example, Delbanco quotes Horace Mann

what those of us who believe strongly in social mobility and in giving every child the opportunity to live a rewarding life want to believe. There is, of course, also strong evidence that improving educational attainment for all Americans, not just those who have grown up in privileged circumstances, is of overriding importance for economic growth—and, beyond that, for strengthening, or at least maintaining, a social fabric that is based in no small measure on the ability of children from every background to move up in life. From the perspective of parents, hope for a better life for one's children, if not for one's self, is of enormous importance in sustaining the "American Dream" and all that that ideal implies for democracy and for at least some

---

as saying, in 1848, that "the spread of education would do more than all things else to obliterate factious distinctions in society," and he also gives a reference to a 1791 statement. Thus, the roots of the argument for social mobility go deep and of course include the Morrill Act. Still, there is no denying that the passage of the GI Bill and the publication of the Truman Commission's six-volume report *Higher Education for American Democracy* (1947) were pivotal events. But it is also important to remember that in the first decades after World War II (really up until the 1960s) American colleges in general did not recruit minority students aggressively, and it is only in more recent years that efforts have been made to enroll more lower-income students. (Richard Kahlenberg of the Century Foundation deserves more credit than anyone else for arguing vigorously and relentlessly for stronger efforts to address disparities by socioeconomic status.) The elite private and public institutions are often criticized for the relatively small number of low- socioeconomic-status (SES) students they enroll, in spite of their stated efforts to do better. We are sure that there is more progress to be made by these institutions, but we also recognize that the real constraint for them is not the pool of well-qualified students from modest backgrounds that they could enroll (which is larger than many of them have recognized) but the extraordinary cross-pressures they face from what must seem like a veritable tidal wave of exceptionally well-qualified students from affluent families. See William G. Bowen, Martin A. Kurzweil, and Eugene M. Tobin, *Equity and Excellence in American Higher Education* (Charlottesville, VA: University of Virginia Press, 2005), for a lengthy discussion of these issues within the elite sector of higher education. The real "action" needs to occur within the much larger sectors that enroll far more students. We are indebted to Eugene Tobin for his help with this discussion of social mobility.

semblance of a national unity that crosses lines of race, ethnicity, and wealth.[45]

Aggregative Data

It is surprisingly difficult to obtain reliable data both on the current extent of disparities in outcomes and on trends. It is obviously important to know whether, however disappointing current disparities may be, we are correcting the problem or allowing it to become worse. Getting the numbers right is crucial, because incorrect (exaggerated) estimates of disparities can be both dangerous in their own right and damaging to the credibility of those of us who want to reduce gaps between rich and poor in educational outcomes. Unfortunately, there have been widely publicized claims by the Pell Institute for the Study of Opportunity in Higher Education that "99 percent of those college students who grew up in the top income quartile went on to complete their BA, compared to 21 percent in the poorest quartile." As Chingos and Dynarski observe: "To put it bluntly, these statistics are wrong." They are based on data from the Current Population Survey that were incorrectly adjusted for shifts in the fractions of students from different income groups still living at home. (The CPS monthly data present parental income

---

[45] Regrettably, recent increases in inequality and grim job prospects for many have called into question the saliency of the American Dream today. Surveys show that the fraction of the population that continues to believe in it has decreased. See Andrew Ross-Sorkin and Megan Thee-Brennan, "Many Feel American Dream Is Out of Reach, Poll Shows," *New York Times*, December 11, 2014, available at http://dealbook.nytimes.com/2014/12/10/many-feel-the-american-dream-is-out-of-reach-poll-shows/?_r=0. See also Robert D. Putnam, *Our Kids: The American Dream in Crisis* (New York: Simon and Schuster, 2015), and Raj Chetty, Nathaniel Hendren, Patrick Kline, Emmanuel Saez, and Nicholas Turner, "Is the United States Still a Land of Opportunity? Recent Trends in Intergenerational Mobility," *American Economic Review* 104, no. 5 (May 2014): 141–47.

data for young adults only if they are still living at home, as many 24-year-olds are not.) Such alleged findings fail to pass the most rudimentary "smell tests." Should we believe that 99 percent of any population achieve this kind of educational outcome? Of course not. Chingos and Dynarski end their piece by warning consumers of data: "If a statistic seems wildly wrong, it probably is."[46]

Far more reliable data are produced by the periodic longitudinal studies conducted by the Department of Education—which, however, are produced too infrequently to generate a reliable time series. In any event, thanks to the recently released study of characteristics and histories of a representative sample of fifteen thousand individuals who were high school sophomores in 2002 and who were tracked for some ten years thereafter (through 2012), we now have a good sense of what has happened to relatively recent cohorts of students from different backgrounds in terms of their socioeconomic status (SES).[47]

The evidence is striking—and very troubling. We see from figure 2 that 60 percent of students from families in the top SES quartile had earned BAs (or higher degrees) by 2012 as com-

---

[46] Matthew M. Chingos and Susan M. Dynarski, "How Can We Track Trends in Educational Attainment by Parental Income? Hint: Not with the Current Population Survey," *Brown Center Chalkboard*, Brookings Institution, Washington, DC, March 12, 2015. Chingos and Dynarski point out that the method used by the Pell team to adjust for changes in numbers of 24-year-olds living at home produced estimates indicating that "more than 110 percent of some groups had completed college—a red flag that this approach has gone off the rails." The Pell Institute authors subsequently issued an "updated report" that remedied this error (www.pellinstitute.org/ publications-Indicators_of_Higher_Education_Equity_in_the_United_States_45_ Year_Report.shtml).

[47] See Institute of Education Sciences (IES), "Postsecondary Attainment: Differences by Socioeconomic Status," *The Condition of Education—Spotlights*, 2015. This study is officially "The Educational Longitudinal Study of 2002," or ELS:2002.

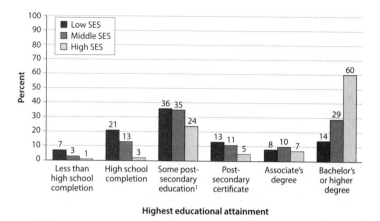

FIGURE 2: Percentage Distribution of Highest Level of Educational Attainment of Spring 2002 High School Sophomores in 2012, by Socioeconomic Status (SES)

Source: National Center for Education Statistics, "Education Longitudinal Study of 2002" (ELS:2002), Base Year and Third Follow-up. See Institute of Education Sciences, *Digest of Education Statistics, 2014*, (Washington, DC), table 104.91, available at https://nces.ed.gov/programs/digest/2014menu_tables.asp.

Note: Students' SES is based on their parents' education and occupation as well as the family income in 2002 and is measured by a composite score on these variables. The "low" SES group is the lowest quartile, the "middle" SES group is the middle two quartiles, and the "high" SES group is the upper quartile. The highest level of educational attainment is that self-reported by participants. High school completion includes GEDs. Detail may not sum to totals because of rounding.

[1] Includes education at any type of postsecondary institution but with no earned postsecondary credential.

pared with just 14 percent of students from the bottom SES quartile and 29 percent of students from families in the middle two SES quartiles. What explains this dramatic pattern? One hypothesis is that differing expectations about college are driving the bus. Fortunately, the ELS:2002 study collected relevant information on this question. In 2002 (when these students were sophomores in high school), 59 percent of students from the low SES quartile expected to earn a BA or higher degree; the corresponding percentage for students from the two middle SES quartiles was 71 percent; 88 percent of students from the high SES quartile expected to earn a BA or higher degree. So, yes, lower educational expectations explain some of the gap in outcomes but hardly all of it. The relatively high level of expectations among sophomores from modest backgrounds (with well over half expecting to earn at least a BA) will surprise many.

It is useful to calculate the difference between measures of expectations and outcomes. We find that the percentage expecting receipt of a BA or higher degree exceeded the actual percentage earning a BA or higher degree by 45 points for the low SES quartile (59 versus 14), by 42 points for the middle SES quartiles (71 versus 29), and by 28 points for the high SES quartile (88 versus 60).

A second hypothesis is that low-SES students, despite their high expectations, had qualifications too weak to allow them to succeed. Could it be that the explanation for the disparities in outcomes is simply the result of different qualifications, especially in math? Again, the Institute of Education Sciences (IES) has data that provide at least a provisional answer to this question. Students' proficiency on a standardized math test was measured when these students were sophomores. The differences in math proficiency, seen in relation to degree earned, are plotted in figure 3.

Not surprisingly, we find that high-SES students scored better on the math proficiency test than did students from lower SES quartiles. But what is much more striking than this finding is that low-SES students who placed in the highest math achievement quartile were far less likely to earn at least a BA than were high-SES students who also placed in the highest math quartile (41 percent versus 74 percent). Another telling comparison

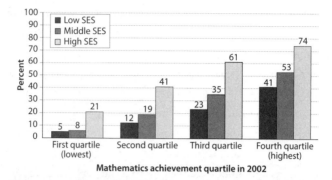

FIGURE 3: Percentage of Spring 2002 High School Sophomores Who Earned a Bachelor's Degree or Higher by 2012, by Socioeconomic Status (SES) and Mathematics Achievement Quartile in 2002

Source: National Center for Education Statistics, "Education Longitudinal Study of 2002" (ELS:2002), Base Year and Third Follow-up. See Institute of Education Sciences, *Digest of Education Statistics, 2014*, (Washington, DC), table 104.91, available at https://nces.ed.gov/programs/digest/2014menu_tables.asp.

Note: Students' SES is based on their parents' education and occupation as well as the family income in 2002 and is measured by a composite score on these variables. The "low" SES group is the lowest quartile, the "middle" SES group is the middle two quartiles, and the "high" SES group is the upper quartile. Mathematics achievement quartiles reflect students' scores on assessments conducted in 2002.

shows that high-SES students who placed in only the second math-proficiency quartile were just as likely to earn at least a BA degree as were low-SES students who placed in the highest math-proficiency quartile (41 percent in each category earning BAs or higher). Finally, it is worth noting that 21 percent of high-SES students who placed in the lowest math proficiency quartile earned at least a BA (as compared with 5 percent of low-SES students). Conclusion: "Put bluntly, class trumps ability when it comes to college graduation."[48]

[48] These are Susan Dynarski's words in commenting on the ELS:2002 study. See her column "For the Poor, the Graduation Gap Is Even Wider than the Enrollment Gap," *The Upshot, New York Times*, June 2, 2015.

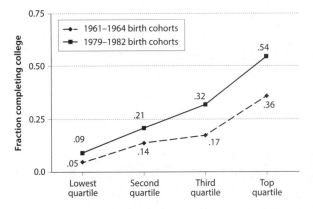

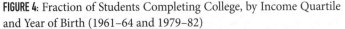

FIGURE 4: Fraction of Students Completing College, by Income Quartile and Year of Birth (1961–64 and 1979–82)

Source: Authors' calculations based on data from US Bureau of Labor Statistics *National Longitudinal Survey of Youth*, 1979 and 1997 (Washington, DC), available at www.nlsinfo.org/content/cohorts/nlsy79 and www.nlsinfo.org/content/cohorts/nlsy97.

The next key question is whether disparities in educational attainment related to SES are becoming ever larger or whether at least some progress is being made in reducing gaps. As we have already said, available data do not allow us to construct a reliable time series, and it is therefore impossible to answer this question with any precision. However, Bailey and Dynarski have shown that disparities in graduation rates by income quartile have not only persisted between the late 1970s and the early years of this century; they have widened (see figure 4).[49]

This powerful figure reveals two truths: (1) pronounced disparities in educational attainment rates by income quartile are all too evident in *both* the 1961–64 birth cohort and the 1979–

---

[49] Martha J. Bailey and Susan M. Dynarski, "Gains and Gaps: Changing Inequality in U.S. College Entry and Completion," NBER Working Paper 17633, December 2011, figure 3. (We reproduce this figure here as figure 4.)

83 cohort, and (2) the disparities between those in the top and bottom income quartiles are appreciably greater in the more recent cohort (54 − 09 = 45 points versus 36 − 05 = 31 points). Because the more recent ELS:2002 study uses SES quartiles (constructed by the Department of Education from "parents' occupation, highest level of education, and income"[50]) rather than the simpler income-only definition of quartiles employed by Bailey and Dynarski, it takes a leap of faith to compare results. If we make the Herculean assumption (probably not too far from the truth) that the top income quartile (Bailey and Dynarski) and the top SES quartile (ELS:2002) are roughly comparable, and if we do not claim precision in making comparisons, we find that the results of the most recent longitudinal study and the previous one (focused on the 1979–82 birth cohorts) are amazingly similar in their contours. To be specific, the ELS:2002 study finds a gap in the attainment of a BA or better between the top and bottom SES quartiles of 46 percentage points (60 versus 14), and the previous study of the 1979 and 1982 birth cohorts found a gap of 45 points (54 versus 9) between the top and bottom income quartiles. These data certainly offer no evidence that the attainment gap is closing—and we suspect, on the basis of impressionistic evidence, that it is continuing to grow.[51]

---

[50] IES, "Postsecondary Attainment," p. 1.

[51] Compounding the greater disparities in graduation rates are increased disparities in time-to-degree. As we have already observed, the study by Bound, Lovenheim, and Turner comparing outcomes between the NELS-72 and NELS-88 cohorts found that increases in time-to-degree were localized among those who began postsecondary education at public colleges outside the most selective universities (the non–top 50 publics). In addition, increases in time-to-degree were most marked among low-income students. See Bound, Lovenheim, and Turner, "Increasing Time to Baccalaureate Degree."

The Virginia Case Study

Cutbacks in state funding seem clearly to have exacerbated existing disparities in outcomes. A meticulous and under-appreciated study of what has happened in Virginia is most revealing.[52] This study of trends in net costs and their effects on students from various income quartiles shows that net costs have risen fastest for the lowest-income students. Between 2007 and 2012, net costs grew at rates of 3.5 percent per year above inflation for students in the first (bottom) income quintile at four-year institutions, as compared with rates of 3.2 percent and 2.6 percent for students in the third and fifth quintiles, respectively; in sharp contrast, prior to 2007 net costs grew fastest for the highest-income students and stayed almost flat for the poorest students. The study also found that fewer than 25 percent of the lowest-income students at public institutions in Virginia went to a four-year institution, as compared with more than 90 percent of students in the highest income quintile—a disturbing pattern in light of the fact that, as we have already noted, much research demonstrates that more or less comparable students enrolling at two-year institutions are far less likely to earn a BA, even if that is their intention, than are students who start at four-year institutions.[53]

---

[52] Virginia provides the grist for an unusually valuable case study, in large part because it has a finely grained longitudinal database. This database, built up by the State Council of Higher Education in Virginia (SCHEV), contains year-to-year records of more than 1.4 million individual students who enrolled in public institutions in the state between the 1997–98 and 2012–13 academic years, including both those who persisted and those who transferred or dropped out. There is, to our knowledge, no other statewide database that is anything like this rich in detail. For a careful analysis of the use of this database, see the hundred-page report by Mulhern et al., "The Effects of Rising Student Costs in Higher Education."

[53] See Bridget T. Long and Michal Kurlaender, "Do Community Colleges Provide a Viable Pathway to a Baccalaureate Degree?" *Educational Evaluation and Policy Analysis* 15, no. 1 (2015): 30–53. See also Bowen, Chingos, and McPherson, *Crossing the Finish Line.*

Moreover, the Virginia study shows that even those students from lower-income families who do enroll in four-year institutions are appreciably less likely than their higher-income peers to remain enrolled and to graduate; since the 1990s, the first-year retention rate for students in the bottom income quintile has been about 11 percentage points lower than the retention rate for their peers in the top income quintile. Finally, careful econometric analysis of these data, controlling for most relevant variables, demonstrates that increases in net costs have had a statistically significant negative effect on student success and that the effect is largest for the poorest students.

This is far from a pretty picture. There is every reason to believe that the situation is essentially the same in many other states—even though no other state has longitudinal data at the level of the individual student that would permit as careful an analysis of relationships and trends (including especially the differential effects on students from poor and "near-poor" families) as is possible in Virginia.[54] It is easy for state authorities to claim—and perhaps even to believe—that Pell Grants and other forms of student aid have protected lower-income students from the effects of state cutbacks in funding, but we know that this is not true in Virginia. And we are highly skeptical that careful analysis would support such claims in many other states.

Implications

The MIT economist David Autor reminds us that, contrary to what he calls "conventional civic mythology," America has not been, and is not, anything like the "land of opportunity" that we

---

[54] Available data suggest that Virginia is not atypical, and, in the words of the Ithaka S+R study by Mulhern, Spies, and Staiger, it "seems to be a microcosm of the higher education scene in the country" (9–10).

are inclined to claim it is. We follow Autor in sorting out three different dimensions of intergenerational economic mobility that are easily confused. First, in international comparisons the United States "has both the lowest mobility and highest inequality among all wealthy democratic countries." However, Autor finds (surprisingly) little evidence that mobility as conventionally measured (likelihood of children moving to a different income quintile from the one their parents have been in) has changed in the United States—at least not yet.[55] But there is a third factor, a subtle but very important one, that Autor notes: even though mobility is very low but not so far falling, income inequality keeps rising throughout the income distribution. What this means is that the "stakes" of moving across quintiles have risen. Concretely, the life of a "near-poor" person in the second quintile of income is significantly worse, compared to that of a "middle-class" person in the third quintile, than it used to be. As Alan Krueger has put it in a telling metaphor, you still have the same (pretty small) chance of climbing the economic ladder, but the rungs on the ladder are farther apart.

This allows Autor to conclude that, despite the absence of a slowdown in (the already low) degree of mobility across generations, "lifetime relative disadvantage of children born to low- versus high-income families has increased substantially."[56] As one of our

[55] For a forceful argument that we are on the brink of a major drop in intergenerational mobility, see Putnam, *Our Kids*.

[56] "Skills, Education, and the Rise of Earnings Inequality," pp. 848–49. Autor writes that, contrary to conventional civic mythology, US intergenerational mobility is relatively low (compared to other countries). In one sense, this is not surprising, because countries with high returns to education (such as the United States) tend to have relatively low mobility for the simple reason that educational attainment is highly persistent within families. Well-off families can afford to invest heavily in the educational preparation of their children, which is a principal reason why children of higher income families do so well in the competition for places in selective

colleagues (former Chancellor William E. Kirwan of the University System of Maryland) puts it: "Absent greater participation and completion rates by the poor, we will have recreated (if we have not already) the economic caste system many of our ancestors left England to escape." More recently, in his "exit interview" with *Inside Higher Ed* staff, Chancellor Kirwan stated what many of us believe:

> I worry a lot about the economic disparity of college completion based on family income. The greatest social problem facing our country is this disparity and what the consequences are as a nation.... What is America? America is the land of opportunity, the upwardly mobile society. We are that no more. It rings hollow. Our nation and our universities have got to come to grips with this problem, and I don't think enough is being done to address this issue.[57]

Achieving Affordability

Important as it is to improve educational outcomes—and it is very important, indeed essential—this must be accomplished without unduly increasing educational costs and, ideally, re-

---

colleges and universities. It is of course well known that disparities in life chances have their roots very early in the lives of children. A Russell Sage book, *Too Many Children Left Behind* (2015), documents the extent to which differences in circumstances at early ages have profound effects all through life. More vigorous efforts should be made to address these early-in-life disparities, but awareness of this problem does not excuse lack of effort at the college level to do what can be done there. As a country, we cannot afford to wait for improvements in childhood education and upbringing to close later-life disparities. We need to press for improved effectiveness at all levels of education—reinforcing the need to ensure that spending on higher education is well-focused on the most important challenges and needs.

[57] Kellie Woodhouse, "A Career's Worth of Change," *Inside Higher Ed*, July 14, 2015, available at www.insidehighered.com/news/2015/07/14/exit-interview-outgoing-university-system-maryland-chancellor-brit-kirwan.

straining the rate of increase in costs for institutions as well as for individuals. Unfortunately, there is a deep-seated aversion in academia to considering costs, as Clark Kerr noted years ago: "The call for effectiveness in the use of resources will be perceived by many inside the university world as the best current definition of evil."[58] Near the end of part III, we return to this "aversion" and suggest an approach to re-engineering the instructional process that depends on both taking advantage of technological advances and re-thinking some principles of shared governance.

It is equally important to recognize that some kinds of education are inherently expensive. Residential college education is an example. The use of highly trained faculty to provide face-to-face instruction in small group settings and the emphasis at some colleges on directed study that includes training undergraduate students to do research is bound to be costly. So, too, is the provision of many kinds of valuable student services needed to encourage low-income students, in particular, to graduate.[59] Advanced training in complex fields is bound to be resource-intensive. In seeking to control costs, the value of these kinds of intensive educational experiences, to the individual and to society, must be kept in mind. Which is not to say that we should fail to look for ways to deliver these kinds of educational experiences as efficiently as possible. Moreover, we should strive to ensure that these exceptional opportunities are allocated according to

[58] See Clark Kerr, *The Uses of the University*, 4th ed. (the Godkin Lectures on the Essentials of Free Government and the Duties of the Citizen), Cambridge, MA: Harvard University Press, 1995, p. 181.
[59] See William G. Bowen, *Higher Education in the Digital Age* (Princeton, NJ: Princeton University Press, 2013). Specifically, see the John Hennessy Discussion, pp. 116–17.

students' ability to take the best advantage of them rather than on the basis of their families' wealth.

Trends in Tuition and Net Costs

Our concern here, however, is not so much with the important need to control institutional costs as it is with the companion problem of rising costs for students and their families. As we emphasized in the prologue, the direct costs of education incurred by colleges and universities cannot be made somehow to disappear, whatever financing mechanisms are chosen. (There are also, of course, the often large opportunity costs borne by students who could have done something else—perhaps working at a full-time job—instead of going to school.) The direct institutional costs of education have to be covered by someone, and a key question is whether higher education is affordable today for those who are being asked to pay for it. Addressing this question involves dealing with both realities and myths. Separating the two is not easy, especially as we approach another presidential campaign that is sure to be marked by much sloganeering.

In examining the aggregate picture, and superimposing it on the more detailed picture for Virginia that we presented earlier, a good place to start is by examining data assembled laboriously by the College Board.[60] Published data on tuition and fees (sometimes called the "sticker price") are shown for 2015–16 in table 1. As is evident, there are considerable differences by sector, with "average" tuition and fees (enrollment-weighted) ranging

---

[60] See Sandy Baum and Jennifer Ma, *Trends in College Pricing 2015* (New York: College Board). To its great credit, the College Board collects and publishes a veritable mountain of data on tuition, net prices, and student aid—all broken down by sector of higher education. We can present only a tiny slice of these data here.

TABLE 1. Average Published Charges (Enrollment-Weighted) for Full-Time Undergraduates by Sector, 2015–16

	Public Two-Year In-District	Public Four-Year In-State	Public Four-Year Out-of-State	Private Nonprofit Four-Year	For-Profit
Tuition and Fees					
2015–16	$3,435	$9,410	$23,893	$32,405	$15,610
2014–15	$3,336	$9,145	$23,107	$31,283	$15,160
$ Change	$99	$265	$786	$1,122	$450
% Change	3.0%	2.9%	3.4%	3.6%	3.0%
Room and Board					
2015–16	$8,003	$10,138	$10,138	$11,516	—
2014–15	$7,856	$9,786	$9,786	$11,162	—
$ Change	$147	$352	$352	$354	—
% Change	1.9%	3.6%	3.6%	3.2%	—
Tuition and Fees and Room and Board					
2015–16	$11,438	$19,548	$34,031	$43,921	—
2014–15	$11,192	$18,931	$32,893	$42,445	—
$ Change	$246	$617	$1,138	$1,476	—
% Change	2.2%	3.3%	3.5%	3.5%	—

Source: The College Board, *Annual Survey of Colleges* (New York).

Notes: Prices in Table 1 are not adjusted for inflation. Prices reported for 2014–15 have been revised and may differ from those reported in *Trends in College Pricing 2014*. Public two-year room and board charges are based on commuter housing and food costs. Tuition and fee figures for the for-profit sector should be interpreted with caution because of the low response rate.

Enrollment-weighted tuition and fees weight the price charged by each institution by the number of full-time undergraduate students enrolled in fall 2014. Public four-year in-state charges are weighted by total fall 2014 full-time undergraduate enrollment in each institution, including both in-state students and out-of-state students. Out-of-state tuition and fees are computed by adding the average in-state price to the out-of-state premium weighted by the number of full-time out-of-state undergraduate students enrolled at each institution. Room and board charges are weighted by the number of undergraduate students residing on campus for four-year institutions and by the number of commuter students for public two-year institutions.

Blanks (marked as "—") indicate that the sample size is too small for reliable estimation.

from just over \$32,400 at private non-profit four-year institutions to just over \$9,400 for in-state students at public four-year institutions and roughly \$3,400 at public two-year institutions.[61] Room and board adds something like \$10,000 to these figures for residential students attending four-year institutions. There is (properly) also great interest in rates of increase over the past three decades or so. An excellent snapshot of trends is provided by another College Board compilation (figure 5).

We see at once that inflation-adjusted tuition and fees at both public and private institutions went up at almost exactly the same rate between 1984–85 and 2000, when a major divergence began: charges at private four-year nonprofit institutions have stayed on almost exactly the same path since then (rising at an average compound rate of 2.46 percent per year), whereas charges at public four-year institutions began to rise appreciably faster in 2000 and have increased at a compound rate of almost 4 percent per year between 1984–85 and 2015–16 (faster than that since 2000). As we discuss in detail later, reductions in state support have been the most important factor driving tuition up at public universities.

How worried we should be about this trend depends on many factors, including of course trends in student aid, which we examine shortly. Another key variable is trends in family income, and a disturbing fact is that the United States is still in a period marked by what economists have called "wage stagna-

---

[61] There are, of course, differences within each of these broad sectors, and the College Board also presents figures by Carnegie Classification (p. 11, table 1B), which show that tuition and fees are highest at the "doctoral" institutions within the private four-year sector (\$40,500, or roughly \$8,000 more than the average for the entire four-year private sector).

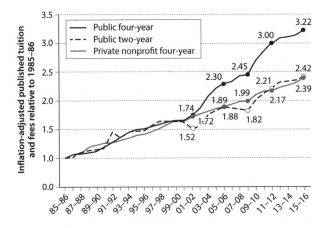

FIGURE 5: Inflation-Adjusted Published Tuition and Fees Relative to 1985–86, 1985–86 to 2015–16

Sources: College Board, *Annual Survey of Colleges* (New York, 2015); National Center for Education Statistics; The Integrated Postsecondary Education Data System.

Notes: The figure shows published tuition and fees by sector, adjusted for inflation, relative to 1985–86 published prices. For example, a value of 3.22 indicates that the tuition and fee price in the public four-year sector in 2015–16 is 3.22 times as high as it was in 1985–86 after adjusting for increases in the Consumer Price Index. Average tuition and fees reflect in-district charges for public two-year institutions and in-state charges for public four-year institutions.

tion."[62] As many commentators have noted, increases in income have been concentrated in the by-now-notorious "top 1 percent" of families grouped by income, whereas wages for the broad "middle class" have, indeed, stagnated. This growing inequality is, in our view, a serious national problem—albeit one that is outside the purview of this study.[63] But the phenomenon is

[62] See Lawrence Michel, "Causes of Wage Stagnation," Economic Policy Institute, Washington, DC, January 6, 2015, available at www.epi.org/publication/causes-of-wage-stagnation/.

[63] For an extended discussion of this problem and one scholar's suggestions as to how we might address it, see Joseph E. Stiglitz, *Rewriting the Rules of the American*

directly relevant in that increases in tuition and fees for all but the most affluent would seem much less onerous if their incomes were increasing as rapidly, or more rapidly, than college costs. We continue to be surprised by how little attention is given to this aspect of the affordability problem—especially by those who choose to assign blame almost exclusively to educational institutions.[64]

Taking account of student aid is very important but is complicated by differences between "dependent" and "independent" students (the former still part of a family unit headed by parents) as well as differences among dependent students in different family income quartiles. We begin by focusing attention on dependent students who attend either an in-state public institution or some type of private institution (either not-for-profit or for-profit). This group of "traditional-age" students predominate at four-year public and at not-for-profit private institutions, with independent students making up less than 20 percent of enrollment at public four-year and less than 15 percent at private not-for-profit institutions.

Table 2 summarizes information about the average tuition charge ("full tuition") facing dependent students from families with differing income levels at various categories of institutions, as well as the "net tuition" families actually have to pay annu-

---

Economy: An Agenda for Growth and Shared Prosperity (New York: W. W. Norton, November 2015).

[64] A welcome exception to this lack of emphasis on the importance of national trends in earnings is James L. Doti, "In Praise of Federal Loans for College," *Chronicle of Higher Education*, July 21, 2015, available at http://chronicle.com/article/In-Praise-of-Federal-Loans-for/231505?cid=megamenu. Doti, president of Chapman University, spells out in detail how stagnating incomes have affected attitudes toward college costs and student debt at private colleges such as his own.

TABLE 2. Full and Net Tuition and Fees ($), by Income Quartile for In-State Dependent Students, by Type of Institution, 2011–12 Academic Year

Income quartiles	Public 2-year		Public 4-year		Private NFP 4-year		For-profit institutions	
	Full T&F	Net T&F	Full T&F	Net T&F	Full T&F	Net T&F	Full T&F	Net T&F
Lowest quartile	2,610	−3,080	7,390	−2,320	27,800	4,970	17,630	11,300
Second quartile	2,850	−310	7,970	1,440	28,960	8,610	17,930	13,720
Third quartile	2,950	1,900	8,150	5,350	29,360	13,970	19,290	18,040
Highest quartile	2,870	2,050	8,620	6,330	32,210	19,720	19,330	17,460

Source: Calculated from National Center for Education Statistics, *National Postsecondary Student Aid Study,* 2012 (Washington, DC).

Note: In-state tuition and fees (T&F) are reported for public institutions; tuition and fees for all institutions are reported for private not-for-profit (NFP) and for-profit institutions.

ally after allowing for the grants and scholarships they receive.[65] A glance at table 2 makes it clear that scholarships and grants make the average "net" tuition students and families actually pay substantially lower than the "sticker price," an effect that is generally larger for students from lower-income families. In fact, at public two-year colleges, average dependent students from families with incomes below the median wind up with *negative* net tuition—they receive enough grant money to fully offset tuition with something left over to help pay living expenses. Indeed, even at public four-year institutions, where the sticker

[65] About 13 percent of public four-year institution attendees go out of state; these students typically face full and net tuition prices similar to those at private not-for-profit institutions.

price is substantially higher than at public two-year colleges, the average student in the bottom income quartile receives free net tuition plus more than $2,000 to put toward room and board.[66] Independent students, who make up 42 percent of enrollment at public two-year colleges and who tend to have a high level of financial need, also face a negative net price on average—it was −$1,810 in 2011–12.

Federal Pell Grants and GI Bill benefits make up a large share of student aid for low-income students at public institutions and at for-profit institutions, but while lower-income students at not-for-profit colleges receive these grants too, they also receive substantial grants and scholarships from other sources, principally the institutions themselves, transforming a $27,800 sticker price to the $4,970 net tuition that families from the lowest income quartile actually have to pay.

Much financial aid goes to high-need students, but those whose families are in the top two quartiles also receive student aid. This is notably the case at private not-for-profit institutions, where, on average, students from top-income-quartile families get a discount of more than $12,000, even though they still wind up having to pay nearly $20,000 per year.

Not to be neglected are the for-profit colleges, which accounted for about 9 percent of students as of the spring of 2013.[67] Even

---

[66] The public four-year sector enrolled, overall, 44 percent of all full-time-equivalent students in 2013–14, and public two-year institutions enrolled another 26 percent; these public four-year and two-year institutions are by far the most important in terms of student numbers. See College Board, *Trends in Student Aid 2014*, New York, pp. 19. Popular journalism has an unfortunate tendency to pay more attention to the Harvards of this world than one should.

[67] NCES, *Digest of Education Statistics, 2014* (Washington, DC), table 307–10, https://nces.ed.gov/programs/digest/d14/tables/dt14_307.10.asp?current=yes.

students from the lowest-income families are expected to come up with a quite substantial tuition payment of over $11,000 after allowing for the student aid grants (mainly Pell Grants and GI Bill benefits) they receive. The same is true of independent students, who make up a whopping 77 percent of the enrollment at for-profit colleges and who are asked, on average, to pay $9,060 net of aid. A large fraction of for-profit college students cover those tuition payments by borrowing, largely through government programs. It is striking that among students who completed certificate programs of two years or less in 2011–12, 65 percent of those at community colleges emerged debt-free, as compared with only 14 percent of for-profit college completers.[68]

These aggregative data lead us to highlight three points:

1. Hard as it is for some families to understand what is, to be sure, a complex system, *there is a huge difference between sticker price and net price*; many colleges and universities, especially the seemingly most expensive ones, are in fact much more affordable than many families realize, often more affordable than institutions with lower sticker prices that have less financial aid to offer. This is true in many instances not only for the most disadvantaged families in the bottom quartile but for those in the second quartile as well. This said, we recognize that perceptions sometimes matter as much as realities.

2. There is obviously a considerable amount of need-based grant aid being distributed by the federal government, by states, and by institutions themselves, and students from

---

[68] College Board, *Trends in Student Aid 2014*, figure 15B. (This table was *not* updated in the 2015 report.)

poorer families are clearly being helped more by financial aid than other students—as they should be.

3. Even so, there is a sizeable gap between sticker price and net price, not only for poor students but also for students from families in the upper quartile of the income distribution attending expensive institutions—which certainly suggests that a non-trivial amount of financial aid is going to those who could presumably attend college without so much help. A recent analysis shows that just over half (51 percent) of the financial aid private four-year institutions award to students from families whose incomes exceed $155,000 per year (about 17 percent of students at such institutions) exceeds their demonstrated financial need. Cutting back on such no-need or "merit" aid could free significant resources for other purposes, including providing more aid to high-need students.[69] The subject of "merit aid" is a sensitive one that we discuss in part III of the book.

In spite of their virtues, the data assembled through the determined efforts of people associated with the College Board suffer from the fact that they are "averages," and averages can obscure, for example, effects of cutbacks in state funding on different categories of students (including the "near-poor") and cause public officials, among others, to discount the longer-term effects of increases in net price. This is why the Virginia study, which we summarized briefly in the previous discussion of disparities in outcomes, is so important. It has the great advantage of being based on an enormous quantity of student-

---

[69] Baum and Jennifer Ma, *Trends in College Pricing 2015*.

level data. To recapitulate, this study shows that, in spite of efforts to offset cuts in public appropriations with increases in student aid, net costs in that state have risen for all students, especially for the lowest-income students—with predictable behavioral effects.

Student Debt

It is mounting student debt that, in the minds of many people, raises the most serious questions about affordability. Of course, levels of debt have to be thought about in relation to the high rates of return earned by many students on these investments (discussed earlier); it is one thing to borrow while anticipating a zero rate of return and quite another to borrow in anticipation of earning a 10 percent return.

There is no denying, however, that debt is a real concern for many students and their families—especially because returns are inevitably uncertain. Still, it is easy to exaggerate the extent of the problem—as all too many journalists do.[70] To cut to the proverbial bottom line, according to recent data, 61 percent of all bachelor's degree recipients at public and private non-profit four-year institutions graduated with some debt. The average amount of debt per borrower was $26,900, and the average amount of debt per graduate was $16,300. Graduate students were more likely to borrow, and to borrow larger amounts of money—but the patterns vary so much by field of study that they cannot be summarized easily.[71]

---

[70] See David Leonhardt, "The Reality of Student Debt Is Different From the Clichés," *The Upshot, New York Times*, July 24, 2014, available at www.nytimes.com/2014/06/24/upshot/the-reality-of-student-debt-is-different-from-the-cliches.html?_r=0&abt=0002&abg=0.

[71] College Board, *Trends in Student Aid 2015*, New York, p. 24.

Much debt is, of course, repaid, and a key question is how much debt is still outstanding. A number that is easily understood is how many education borrowers there are today with less than $10,000 of outstanding debt (for both undergraduate and graduate study): the number is 39 percent; another 28 percent of borrowers owe between $10,000 and $25,000, and 4 percent owe $100,000 or more. Most of those with large amounts of debt incurred it during graduate study, with many pursuing degrees in presumptively well-paying fields such as medicine and business.[72]

Trends are also less frightening than much commentary suggests. Data compiled by the Federal Reserve Bank of New York show that, over the ten years between 2004 and 2014, inflation-adjusted education debt per borrower increased by just 39 percent.[73] With regard to default rates, the College Board reports that in 2014–15, 14 percent of borrowers with federal student loans defaulted on their loans, accounting for 9 percent of the total outstanding debt: "Default rates ranged from 21% for public two-year colleges and 19% for for-profit institutions to 9% for public four-year colleges and universities and 7% for four-year private nonprofit institutions."[74] Adam Looney of the Treasury Department and Constantine Yannelis of Stanford, in examining newly released data, estimate that 75 percent of the increase in defaults between 2004 and 2011 can be explained by

---

[72] See ibid., pp. 4, 22. This study also reports that the percentage of borrowers enrolled in income-related repayment plans (which cap annual payments) increased from 14 percent to 20 percent between FY14:Q3 and BY15:Q3 (p. 21).

[73] College Board, *Trends in Student Aid 2015*, p. 28.

[74] Ibid., p. 4. See also Dynarski, "Why Students with the Smallest Debts Have the Larger Problem."

the surge in borrowers at for-profit colleges and (to a lesser extent) at community colleges.[75]

In reviewing the same set of newly released data, Kevin Carey makes the important point that default rates tell only part of the story; non-repayment rates (a result of students deferring obligations to repay) are also relevant and can be much higher. As Carey emphasizes, problems of high rates of default and non-repayment are most acute "when students with very little money attend colleges with very little money," and he cites data for the Historically Black Colleges and Universities to buttress this point.[76] Obviously debt problems are highly concentrated among both certain categories of students and certain types of institutions.

While it is important to place all data on educational debt in context (and not to exaggerate modal situations by emphasizing outliers or by being unclear about where most borrowing occurs), it is also important to recognize that some graduate students, in particular, face serious financial problems in the current environment, even though traditionally graduate students have had low default rates. There is reason to be especially concerned about students with large amounts of debt who have pursued degrees in fields such as the humanities and social services (and, these days, the law) where earning prospects are limited. Individuals have to take responsibility for their own lives, and there is a limit to the value of what others tell them—and to the ability of others to prevent what turns out to be destructive

[75] As quoted by Susan Dynarski in "New Data Gives Clearer Picture of Student Debt," *The Upshot, New York Times*, September 10, 2015.
[76] Kevin Carey, "Student Debt Is Worse than You Think," *New York Times*, October 7, 2015.

behavior.[77] Still, it seems evident that giving students, especially prospective graduate students, realistic assessments of job prospects in the fields in which they are interested should help. It is *not* helpful, however (to say the least), to encourage students to default on debt without understanding the consequences. One of the most irresponsible stories we have seen encourages just such behavior—but fortunately, wiser heads have denounced this advice as very dangerous.[78]

It is also important to recognize that students can borrow too little as well as too much. Our earlier discussion of completion rates and time-to-degree referenced concerns that students may be tempted to work too many hours in order to avoid borrowing—but may end up, as a consequence, taking longer to complete their degrees or not completing them at all. "Penny-wise and pound foolish" is the adage that comes to mind. Students' time is one of their most valuable resources, and it should be husbanded carefully—even if taking out a modest amount of debt is necessary to meet essential expenses.[79] We deal in part III with the growing debate over whether aspiring students should

[77] It is unclear how valuable the rising number of programs (courses) in "financial literacy" really are, but it is encouraging to see that more people are at least interested in the subject. See Beckie Supiano, "Financial Literacy: Can It Be Taught? Should Colleges Even Try?" *Chronicle of Higher Education*, July 17, 2015, available at http://chronicle.com/article/Financial-Literacy-Can-It-Be/231691/.

[78] See Lee Siegel, "Why I Defaulted on My Student Loans," *New York Times*, June 6, 2015, available at www.nytimes.com/2015/06/07/opinion/sunday/why-i-defaulted -on-my-student-loans.html?_r=0. See also Jordan Weissman, "The *New York Times* Should Apologize for the Awful Op-Ed It Just Ran on Student Loans," *Slate*, June 8, 2015, available at www.slate.com/blogs/moneybox/2015/06/08/lee_siegel_new_york _times_op_ed_is_this_the_worst_op_ed_ever_written_about.html.

[79] See Laura W. Perna, "Understanding the Working Student," *Academe*, July–August 2010. Earlier work by Bowen, Chingos, and McPherson, reported in *Crossing the Finish Line* (p. 174), also noted the insidious effects of substituting too many hours of work for modest amounts of debt.

be assured that they can graduate with no debt at all—a highly dubious proposition, in our view.

As we mentioned earlier in a note, Sandeen has argued that affordability is "the biggest issue" facing higher education.[80] Affordability is, to be sure, a serious issue—especially in terms of the potential effects on student behavior. Such effects, which can be the result not only of exaggerated worries but also of demonstrable increases in net tuition, need to be monitored carefully. We also need to recognize the enormous difference in the affordability problem facing students from low-income families who feel obliged to send money home to their families from that facing students with two working parents in middle-class jobs who wrestle with the strains of making mortgage payments and saving for retirement. It is no doubt too soon to assess the longer-term consequences of increasing reliance on loans in higher education finance. But we do not agree with Sandeen that affordability is "the biggest issue" in higher education today. We regard disappointing outcomes, ranging from low completion rates to long time-to-degree, especially among lower-SES students, as even more serious. It is of course true that the issues are linked. In our view, it would be a mistake, nonetheless, to elevate worries over affordability to the top rung of pressing national issues.

Strengthening Leadership Capacities

When we started working on this short book, we did not include "strengthening leadership capacities" on our list of pressing national needs. The more we have worked on this project,

---

[80] See Sandeen, "Here's What I Learned," July 7, 2015.

however, the more convinced we have become that this is a real need—however hard it may be to achieve.[81]

There are, of course, many extremely talented leaders of both educational institutions and their boards, and we certainly do not intend to demean any of them; we only want to argue that they are not the norm and that trends are unfavorable. The great leaders we have had the good fortune to know, as well as those of earlier eras we have read about, share several striking qualities. (We refrain from naming individuals.) These individuals have provided leadership to all of higher education, as well as to the institutions to which they owed their primary loyalty. That is, they have seen themselves as contributors to a larger community. Strong leaders have displayed courage in addressing controversial issues, and, through their own energy and hard work, have enjoyed the strong support of their own academic communities. They have worked in supportive environments that they have focused energy on building. It strikes us that successful presidents have found ways to be "happy warriors," more stimulated by opportunity than brought low by troubles.

The main problem today, as we perceive it, is that many sitting presidents are overly risk-averse. Too often they seem to be, for entirely understandable reasons, reluctant to take unpopular

---

[81] We focus here on leadership at the institutional level, but leadership at the federal and state political levels matters greatly too. Helping to lead public discussion and policy-making toward facing hard challenges like promoting greater educational effectiveness for students from populations that have not traditionally been well served is far more difficult than adopting popular slogans. We do believe that there is the potential for political success through promoting a realistic focus on the hard issues, although we have more confidence in the governing process that happens between elections than in election campaigns as a vehicle for realistic thinking. A valuable contrast between campaigning and governing "mindsets" is Amy Gutmann and Dennis Thompson, *The Spirit of Compromise: Why Governing Demands It and Campaigning Undermines It* (Princeton, NJ: Princeton University Press, 2012).

positions (with faculty, alumni, and legislators). This is especially unfortunate because we believe that new approaches, some fairly radical, may be needed if the pressing national problems we have described earlier are to be addressed.

We are not advocating heroic self-sacrifice on the part of campus leaders. There are, we recognize, situations in which it is just not worth spending valuable capital trying to fix vexing issues that have no clear solutions. To be sure, there are occasions when a resignation on principle is called for—but such occasions are rare. Successful presidents combine the steady nerve to face a tough and truly consequential issue with the resourcefulness and skill to tackle it effectively and then to move on. Our worry is that some leaders are so eager to get past the latest crisis that they fail to make progress on the greater challenges they face.

But before discussing why we believe the need for strong leadership is especially important today, we first focus on what we regard as the factors contributing to the current problem.

First on our list is the difficult economic environment besetting all but the most privileged educational institutions. Like it or not, presidents, their provosts, and other key administrators are forced to confront difficult (unpopular) choices. These are often created by the fact that, at most institutions, revenues, including declining per-student state support at public institutions, have failed to keep pace with pressures to maintain spending levels, if not to spend more. In addition, the stubbornly stagnant wage pattern in the United States for all but the most fortunate has led to heightened resistance to tuition increases—a resistance shared and sometimes insisted upon by state legislators. There also seems to be increasing resistance to even modest reliance on loan finance. Declining public support for higher education in general—notwithstanding increasing desires for degrees and the high returns associated with degree completion—is a further source of stress. A closely related challenge is that political pressures can so easily ensnare leaders—witness the recent uproar associated with the "resignation or firing" of the chancellor of the University of Illinois at Urbana-Champaign.[82] Most recently, racial tensions, along with struggles to defend free speech (even when it is offensive to some) while seeking to maintain respect for individuals of all races, have created pressures on leaders that they cannot always surmount. None of these issues is without precedent, but their intensity and ubiquity these days are striking.

Needless to say, it is much harder to divide up, more or less cheerfully, a shrinking pie than a growing one. Cost pressures have contributed to the growing reliance on adjunct faculty, a development that has often been unsettling to tenure-track and contingent faculty alike. Unavoidable changes in staffing structures inevitably create tensions between faculty and administrators. In private colleges, a desire to preserve or expand enrollments has sometimes led to "beggar-my-neighbor" merit aid competitions that wind up undermining everyone's revenue base (while consuming resources that might otherwise help needy students). Destructive competition can also occur as institutions or different systems within a state vie for legislative support.

We conclude, reluctantly, that there are too many too-small institutions competing for a limited student market. This sec-

---

[82] See Jack Stripling, "Stage Is Set for Uncommon Ugliness in Illinois Chancellor's Exit," *Chronicle of Higher Education*, August 13, 2015, available at http://chronicle.com/article/Stage-Is-Set-for-Uncommon/232379/.

tor might well be more viable with fewer, larger institutions serving the same or a larger total number of students. One consequence is pressure to close individual campuses or even entire institutions—as in the case of Sweet Briar College. As that revealing saga demonstrates all too clearly, the passions unleashed by even well-reasoned efforts to close, in an orderly way, a college faced with what certainly seemed to be unsustainable trends (in enrollment, the discount rate, and the spend rate on unrestricted endowment) can be more than demoralizing—they can be poisonous in the extreme.[83] Closing the college was averted, at the last minute, as a result of a "settlement" brokered by a politically conscious Virginia attorney general, and Sweet Briar will remain open for at least one more year and probably even longer, albeit with a curricular structure, a student population, and a financial profile yet to be defined.

In today's world—with attorney general intervention (in the case of Cooper Union as well as Sweet Briar[84]), county judges also feeling political "heat," and irate alumni able to use social media and PR machinery to generate strong opposition to any potential closing— prolonged death agonies for colleges may be inevitable. Boards have to anticipate intense pressures to "go the last mile" and "spend the last dollar," whether or not there are good reasons for just hanging on. Given this history, what

[83] As noted in the preface, interested readers can consult the much fuller account of both the Sweet Briar saga and vexing issues at Cooper Union by Bacow and Bowen, "Double Trouble."

[84] For a discussion of the problematic role of attorneys general in such situations, see Lawrence S. Bacow and William G. Bowen, "The Real Work of 'Saving' 2 Colleges Has Yet to Be Done," *Chronicle of Higher Education*, September 8, 2015, available at http://chronicle.com/article/The-Real-Work-of-Saving-/232901/?cid=at&utm _source=at&utm_medium=en.

president and what board are likely to vote to close a college before the proverbial "last dog is hung"? Alice Brown, an expert on small colleges faced with pressures to close, has come to essentially the same conclusion. She writes (in personal correspondence): "I fear … that there really is no way to close a college with grace and dignity. Those that 'crash and burn' seem to go as gently 'into that good-night' as any. So sad." Indeed!

There is clearly a collective action problem here. One can at least imagine an effort among a substantial group of colleges that might agree on more orderly mechanisms for managing school closings by, for example, making routine arrangements for helping students relocate, assisting faculty in their own relocation, and even providing technical assistance in the difficult process of managing mergers. Needless to say, none of this would be easy. But however these problems are addressed, the possibility (probability) that more colleges will need to consider closing is just another reason strong leaders for such colleges can be hard to attract.[85]

The rise of the social media has been, we suspect, enormously important in making it possible for dissenters to rally opposition to decisions that they don't like—a disruptive power that has had great influence both for good and for ill in contexts far removed from US higher education, including in national political struggles around the world. Skillful users of the media can marshal opposition quickly and over large geographic territories, as it was much more difficult to do in the days when "snail

---

[85] Moody's Investors Service has issued a sobering report that suggests, in the words of the title of an article by Andy Thomason in the *Chronicle of Higher Education* (September 25, 2015), "Small Colleges' Closure Rate Could Triple by 2017, Moody's Says."

mail" was the primary means of communication. Related is the apparently increasing tendency for political forces (often fueled by social media) to intrude forcefully into the decision-making process facing private as well as public institutions. As we have noted, county judges and attorneys general with political agendas can create pressures on leadership that may seem, and may be, irresistible. This is certainly not to argue that opposition to presidential or board decisions is inherently "bad." Surely not. Vigorous debate and checks and balances are definitely in order. But, as the histories of both Sweet Briar and Cooper Union demonstrate, a balance has to be found that will not discourage capable presidents and boards from accepting and then discharging fiduciary obligations.

Intemperate debates, both in the press and in the courts, over what should happen when an institution is struggling (pointing fingers and playing the "blame game") help explain why capable people may be reluctant to step up to leadership roles in potentially divisive and stressful situations. Rather than confront truly difficult decisions, and risk personal damage, it may often seem easier for both presidents and trustees just to hope that the sun will shine tomorrow—whatever the official weather forecast— and to assume that if it rains eventually, as it almost surely will, it will rain on someone else's parade. While this sort of response may help buy the president a good night's sleep, in the long run repeating this kind of response is likely to lead to a disappointing, if not failing, presidency, and perhaps a diminished institution.

There is a direct connection to a problem we have already noted: the effects of "rocking the boat" on one's chances of being able to move to another leadership position in higher education. Largely as a result of the forces we have enumerated, search committees seem more inclined today than earlier to want to avoid any potentially embarrassing appointment. Thus even a hint that a president or provost may have exhibited "anti-faculty" tendencies in one position may disqualify the individual from consideration by those seeking new leadership. "Just play it safe" seems to be a mantra (though unspoken) that is more powerful than it should be. The derivative effects on presidents or provosts who do not want to think that they are in their last job are easy to imagine. It must be tempting for many such people to just keep their heads down and wait for a sunnier day. These forces can easily inhibit vigorous and, one would hope, fruitful debate over alternative courses of action.

The problems of attracting good leadership under these circumstances are not confined to presidential positions. A recent story titled "Our Leader Left, Who's Left to Lead?" points out, in a specific setting (Atlanta), that it is far from easy to fill important deanships.[86] We all know that in higher education it is notoriously difficult to engage in "management development," but this is surely not the only problem. Faculty with the potential to assume leadership roles may well ask why they should leave what may be reasonably comfortable situations to subject themselves to the kinds of second-guessing and even personal attacks that are all too common.[87]

For the sake of readers who may be contemplating a life in administration, we do not want our candid account of the

---

[86] Nathan Bennet, *Chronicle of Higher Education*, July 22, 2015.

[87] See, for example, Andy Thomason's article in *Inside Higher Ed* (September 25, 2015), " 'Angry Olives' Game Skewers U. of Akron's President," which describes an interactive game in which the president's "cartoon likeness dismantles beloved parts of the campus with an olive-loaded slingshot."

hazards to scare them away. Potentially successful presidents should be neither cowed nor depressed. Resourcefulness, patience, determination—and a lively sense of the absurd—can lead to fulfillment in what remain important and often rewarding jobs.

Why does the need for strong leadership, willing to take risks, matter so much? It is, to be sure, far from a new issue, but it is a building one that has evolved in the wrong ways. Clark Kerr, in looking back on the 1960s from his perspective as chairman of the Carnegie Commission on Higher Education and elder statesman, wrote:

> I would argue for giving leadership a better chance to exert itself. Most successful new policies in higher education have come from the top. *We need to reverse the denigration of leadership....* It was denigrated by students in the late 1960s and early 1970s.... Presidents were used like Kleenex. The institutions survived, but their leaders did not. Yet in a time of troubles, as then loomed and now loom again, leaders are more needed but are harder to get to serve and to keep. To the list of presidential attributes I gave in the original Godkin lectures, I would now add the ability to withstand the frustrations from all of the checks and balances, and the criticism from all of the more active and vocal participants; that is, the possession of nerves like sewer pipes.[88]

Another visionary leader from days gone by, John Gardner, was fond of saying that we need to be spared both "uncritical lovers

[88] Kerr, *The Uses of the University*, p. 137.

and unloving critics."[89] The admonitions of both Kerr and Gardner were true in their days, and they are highly salient now.

Faculty responsibilities in key areas such as vetting the qualifications of colleagues and potential colleagues remain much the same (fortunately) as they have been for over a hundred years. But faculty roles in making resource allocation decisions, which have always been more limited, and in determining teaching methods, need to be re-thought. Advances in technology require investments in teaching technologies and decisions about staffing patterns that more and more often transcend departmental and even institutional boundaries. Aspects of governance structures need to evolve away from vertical models, centered on departments, to horizontal models that focus on achieving a combination of educational effectiveness and cost efficiencies.[90] This requires even stronger leadership in key positions, combined with more real consultation, with faculty and others, than even Kerr envisioned.

"Shared governance" should not be construed as "divided governance," with faculty and administrators arguing over "who owns what." Rather, administrators and faculty need to meet together, around a bigger table, in a genuinely collaborative mode. Presidents need to exert real leadership, and faculty need to contribute the knowledge and the enthusiasm for teaching that they possess.[91]

Absent such leadership, and absent a willingness to engage in real experimentation, which inevitably entails risk-taking, higher

[89] John W. Gardner, "Uncritical Lovers, Unloving Critics," commencement address given at Cornell University, Ithaca, NY, June 1, 1968, published in *Journal of Education Research* 62, no. 9 (May–June 1969).
[90] Bowen and Tobin, *Locus of Authority*, especially pp. 151ff.
[91] Ibid., pp. 205ff.

education is unlikely to take full advantage of technological advances (including "flipped" classrooms, "hybrid" courses that combine online content delivery with face-to-face meetings, and adaptive learning platforms) that offer real promise of improving educational outcomes while controlling costs. At the end of part III we suggest modest ways in which stronger leadership might be encouraged.

PART III

An Agenda for Change

It is essential to be realistic, no matter how powerful nostalgia and reverence for an imagined past may be and however tempting it may be just to assume that brighter days are ahead. We hope that brighter days are indeed ahead, but we need to act so as to make that prospect more rather than less likely. Regrettably, there are no readily discernible silver bullets. But we have identified an "agenda for change" that we believe may at least ameliorate the problems we have described in part II. We have tried to identify pathways toward constructive change without in any way claiming that we have it "all figured out"! In what follows we attempt both to sketch some positive ways of thinking ahead and to debunk some approaches that we do not regard as soundly conceived.

Governmental Funding—Apart from Student Aid

General Propositions

How can governments at both state and federal levels make reasonable and constructive judgments about investing in higher education? Given the current worries about managing the costs of higher education, a good starting point is to distinguish clearly two different dimensions of the topic, namely cost *reduction* and cost *shifting*. Cost reduction refers to the process of increasing the efficiency of producing higher education—that is, getting an equivalent quality of education for less money, whether by reducing overhead costs, introducing new technologies, or whatever. We discuss prospects for improving efficiency shortly. Cost shifting involves reducing the payment burden on one group of citizens by increasing the burden on another group. In too many discussions, the identity of that second group is either passed over in silence or identified vaguely as "the rich."

This is a very important point to have in mind when considering policy choices. Undoubtedly many of the people who believe that their (or their children's) college bills are unaffordable also think that tax increases would be unaffordable. In the current circumstances, there are certainly groups of students who really cannot afford to pay for college, and an important policy goal is to shift the burden away from them. But when the discussion moves toward saying "most" people cannot afford college, as it sometimes does, we are owed a believable answer to the question of who can afford it better. In examining the prospects of solving the college affordability problem by raising taxes at the top of the distribution, we also need to be aware that taxing the rich is the favored solution for addressing other pressing social problems, including poor housing, weak schools, a decaying physical infrastructure, and so on. We shouldn't simply assume that reducing the college cost burden on families in, say, the third quartile of the income distribution has the highest priority.

There is also good reason to be skeptical of extreme solutions to our policy dilemmas—such as "college should be free," on the one hand, and "nobody should pay taxes to support liberal education," on the other. For more than a century, paying for college in the United States has been a shared responsibility of families, governments, and philanthropy. The notion that a large segment of the population would pay the full cost of their offspring's college education entirely from their own resources is foreign to US experience. Equally foreign is the idea that a significant number of families would find the financial burdens of education for their children or themselves (including the burden of covering living expenses while studying full time) completely relieved by funding from government and philanthropy. The terms on which expenses have been shared among these three sources have varied tremendously over time and across students and institutions, but some form of sharing has long been the norm.

We do not think this pattern of sharing will change radically in the foreseeable future. America is too pluralistic, and the provision of higher education too decentralized (and too expensive), to expect the kinds of radical solutions that some may hope for to be implemented. There are, moreover, reasons to feel good about this tradition of shared financing of higher education. Individuals who acquire more education generally benefit economically from doing so and wind up, on the whole, better off than their fellow citizens. It is reasonable for them (and their parents) to share in the cost. Not all the benefits of college accrue to individual graduates, however. There is substantial, and growing, evidence that there are strong network effects and that a community benefits economically from having a more educated population;[1] there is also evidence that persons with more

[1] Enrico Moretti, "Estimating the Social Return to Higher Education: Evidence from Longitudinal and Repeated Cross-Sectional Data," *Journal of Econometrics* 121 (2004): 175–212.

education are more civic-minded.[2] Governments and philanthropies have reason to support institutions that produce these positive externalities.

Finally, it is all too obvious that in a society with massive income inequality, relying solely on families to pay for college is sure to restrict, if not eliminate, college opportunity for the least well off, with results that are both highly unfair and wasteful of valuable human resources. Thus concerns of efficiency (because of externalities) and fairness (because of inequality) argue that government and philanthropy need to have a continuing role in college finance. So we should put aside all-or-nothing solutions to financing higher education and focus instead on the real questions of balance, trade-offs, and affordability (both for families and for governments), which will help determine how productive and how fair our investments in higher education will be.[3]

---

[2] See Thomas Dee, "Are There Civic Returns to Education?" *Journal of Public Economics* 2004, no. 88 (9–10): 1697–1720. See also Sandy Baum, Jennifer Ma, and Kathleen Payea, "*Education Pays 2013: The Benefits of Higher Education for Individuals and Society*" (New York: College Board, 2013).

[3] We intend to keep the focus here mainly on governments and families. Philanthropy, in the form of gifts to colleges and scholarships to individuals, plays a valuable role in the overall system by helping sustain a wide diversity of institutions and by affording exceptional opportunity to some students in distinctive situations. But for most students in our country, the financing of their education will be mainly in the hands of families (whether parents of young adults or, for older students, the students themselves) and governments. The limited role of philanthropy in today's higher education is just one reason to regret ill-informed and poorly reasoned op-eds like Victor Fleischer's in the *New York Times* ("Stop Universities From Hoarding Money," August 19, 2015) objecting to Yale's handling of its endowment. Fleischer seems to think Yale's endowment would grow faster if they made their investments with less well-paid investors and that the world would be better if Yale spent out its endowment at an unsustainable rate. The real problem, though, is that debating these points is a tremendous distraction from the issues that genuinely matter. Questions about how the one hundred best-endowed colleges spend their money are of no consequence to the educational opportunities of the vast majority of

We say "governments" because both state and federal governments have come to play major roles in higher education finance, and these roles take very different forms. Traditionally, states have invested in college education by investing in universities and colleges, that is, by building, owning, and operating colleges (though through governance arrangements that lend universities much more autonomy than typical government agencies enjoy). Traditionally, public universities received the majority of their funds from their owners—state governments—and supplemented those funds with payments for tuition and room and board. The federal government, in contrast, operates only a few, mostly military, colleges and has instead focused its role on supporting undergraduate education by helping students pay for their education through grants and loans. Basically, states give colleges money, and the federal government gives students money. (Of course, the federal government plays a very different, and substantial, role in supporting research and graduate education.) How well this division of labor works, and can be made to work, is a pair of critical questions for the future of US higher education.

The Role of State Governments—and the Federal Government

We increasingly think of public support of higher education as a federal responsibility, but in fact, until the late 1960s the federal government's role was largely limited to support for scientific research at the nation's large universities. It had no continuing role in paying for undergraduate education. Back then, state-run colleges and universities educated over 75 percent of

---

American college students. There is, of course, also a positive case to be made for maintaining healthy endowments. See David Oxtoby, "Endowments Are Financial Pillars, Not Piggy Banks," *Chronicle of Higher Education*, September 21, 2015.

undergraduate students, and the lion's share of funding for their education was paid by state and local governments, almost entirely through appropriations to support the institutions' budgets. In 1969–70, more than half of public university budgets were funded by state and local governments, with tuition from families covering only about 15 percent.[4] By 2012–13, this picture had changed dramatically: tuition (net of student aid) now makes a significantly larger contribution to the revenues of four-year colleges than state and local appropriations do.[5]

Still, it remains true that in-state tuition at public universities remains low in many states. Using state tax revenue to subsidize "college for all" through low in-state tuition is regressive in that taxpayers in general, including those with moderate and low incomes, are covering a large share of the significant costs involved in educating children of affluent families at public universities. This problem is complicated by the political reality that the "elites" who vote and have a disproportionate voice in decision-making are precisely the same group that would be hurt most by shifting costs to higher-income families by raising in-state tuition.

This phenomenon notwithstanding, there has been a striking shift in the relative shares of the cost burden for public higher education from taxpayers to tuition payers, and this shift is a major driver of affordability concerns. It deserves a close look.

Figure 6, showing year-over-year changes in tuition and fees and in state and local funding per student, illustrates how the two trends mirror one another. When state funding has taken

[4] See Michael S. McPherson and Morton O. Schapiro, *The Student Aid Game* (Princeton, NJ: Princeton University Press, 1998), p. 26.
[5] See Sandy Baum and Jennifer Ma, *Trends in College Pricing 2015* (New York: College Board), p. 29, figure 18A.

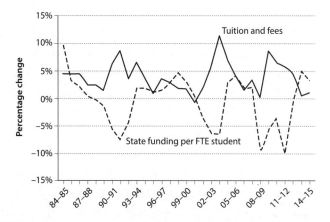

FIGURE 6: Annual Percentage Change in Inflation-Adjusted Per-Student State Funding for Higher Education and in Tuition and Fees at Public Institutions, 1984–85 to 2014–15

Source: Sandy Baum and Jennifer Ma, *Trends in College Pricing 2015* (New York: College Board), p. 27, available at http://rends.collegeboard.org.

an abrupt drop, usually in recessions, tuition charges have shot up, with schools striving to make up the difference. An examination of the year-by-year pattern of changes in state appropriations for higher education over recent decades (using underlying data available from the Spencer Foundation) is also instructive. The story told is straightforward: states' performance in funding higher education is the result of the combination of states' total appropriations to their colleges and universities and the number of students enrolled in those institutions. Thus, at the beginning of the 1990s, slumping state appropriations in the wake of the Savings and Loan Crisis and mild recession led to reductions in appropriations, but the blow was cushioned on a per-student basis by stagnating enrollments. By the end of the 1990s, the dot-com boom allowed appropriations per student to recover most of the ground lost in that decade despite rising enrollments.

The brief but intense recession that began in 2001 slowed appropriations, but the rapid recovery that followed again allowed growth in appropriations to outpace increases in enrollment.

But then, in 2008, for state governments and everyone else, the roof fell in. Between 2007 and 2009, the tax revenues of state governments plummeted with the failing economy, dropping by more than $5 billion at the same time that a declining labor market caused many students to stay in college or return. Public enrollments grew by more than a million students, or over 10 percent, on a full-time-equivalent (FTE) basis. Under the combined pressures of revenue drops and burgeoning enrollments, appropriations per student fell by 15 percent in two years and continued to fall for two more years.

This detailed narrative is worth tracing through for at least two reasons. First, it is apparent how vulnerable states' ability to fund the costs of higher education are to cyclical fluctuations in tax revenues and enrollments. These fluctuations wreak havoc with budgets at both legislative and campus levels. The development of mechanisms that would help stabilize budgets in the face of such fluctuations would allow governments and institutions to plan more effectively and contribute to more efficient operations.[6]

The second big point is that there is nothing in this narrative that suggests that there has been an abrupt and widespread change in state policies toward funding state-run colleges. States

---

[6] See Thomas J. Kane, Peter Orszag, and David L. Gunter, "State Fiscal Constraints and Higher Education Spending: The Role of Medicaid and the Business Cycle," The Urban Institute, available at: http://www.urban.org/sites/default/files/alfresco/publi cation-pdfs/310787-State-Fiscal-Constraints-and-Higher-Education-Spending.PDF, 2003. See also Michael S. McPherson and Morton Owen Schapiro, "Funding Roller Coaster for Public Higher Education," *Science* 302, no. 5648 (2003): 1157.

have responded to circumstances, cutting appropriations when revenues are reduced, restoring cuts when there is capacity to do so. Rather, what the data for the quarter century between 1983 and 2008 suggest is a slow erosion in per-student support as states have roughly sustained their total funding of public higher education but have not kept up with enrollment growth.

TABLE 3. Annual Appropriations per Full-Time-Equivalent (FTE) Student Averaged over Five-Year Intervals, 1983–84 to 2012–13

Interval	Appropriations per FTE
1983–87	$9,727
1988–92	$9,331
1993–97	$8,805
1998–2002	$9,578
2003–07	$8,857
2008–12	$7,505

Source: Authors' calculations based on College Board, *Annual Survey of Colleges* (New York, 2015); Illinois State University, Grapevine Reports; Institute of Education Sciences, *Digest of Education Statistics, 2013* (Washington, DC), table 307.10, available at https://nces.ed.gov/programs/digest/2013menu_tables.asp; National Center for Education; Integrated Postsecondary Education Data System fall 2013 enrollment data.

Notes: Enrollment figures are for fall full-time-equivalent (FTE) enrollments for public two-year and four-year institutions, with fall 2014 estimated at fall 2013 levels. Funding is for both two-year and four-year institutions and includes tax revenues and other state funds for higher education but excludes funding for capital expenditures. Tuition and fees reflect an FTE enrollment-weighted average of two-year and four-year prices.

Table 3 captures this trend by examining five-year averages of state appropriations per FTE student.

In the middle of the decade of the 2000s, states were providing about $900 less per year in inflation-adjusted dollars than they were in the middle of the 1980s—about a 10 percent decline. This reduction of $900 per student may not sound like much in light of today's tuition levels. But, as we discussed earlier when examining affordability, a large fraction of college students have a significant part of their tuition paid by scholarships and grants. In fact, in 2005, tuition paid by students at four-year public institutions, net of these grants and scholarships, averaged less than $2,500 in 2012 dollars.[7] Thus a significant part of the increased money families were contributing in the mid-2000s could be seen as making up for the decline in state funding that took place.

Key Questions

These recent developments in the evolution of state support for public higher education raise three key questions:

1. Will the states be able to recover from the Great Recession as they have from past recessions? In 2013–14, state higher education appropriations summed to $76.2 billion. They had been at $90.5 billion in inflation-adjusted dollars just six years earlier. Even if states succeed in recovering much of that ground as the economy continues to strengthen, there remains the question of how much enrollments will rise, forcing states to stretch their dollars further.

[7] See College Board, *Trends in Student Aid 2014*, figure 12.

In the near term, prospects for revenue growth in the states are reasonably encouraging. Employment and income are up in most states, and therefore major revenue sources—including income taxes, property taxes, and sales taxes—are likely to perform well. In addition, some spending needs, for example, for income support and emergency assistance, are likely to lessen. However, in the slightly longer run, other developments bode ill for state appropriations. In particular, states that chose to participate in the federal Medicaid expansion will begin assuming progressively more of the costs of that commitment. Moody's Analytics, in a study prepared for the National Commission on Financing 21st Century Higher Education, offered this assessment:

> The results of the analysis confirm a dismal outlook for state higher education funding in most states over the next decade.... [In Moody's projection,] national state Medicaid spending increases as a share of overall state spending from 15.6 percent in fiscal 2013, to 17.9 percent by fiscal 2024. In dollar terms, that equates to as much as $60 billion spent on Medicaid over the next decade that previously would have been available for discretionary items such as higher education.[8]

On the other hand, demographic projections of public college enrollment prepared by the US Department of Education offer a somewhat more favorable picture. Following a period from 2000 to 2013 when enrollments rose at an annual rate of about 1.9 percent, federal projections now suggest a somewhat

[8] Dan White, *Crowded Out: The Outlook for State Higher Education Spending*, April 21, 2015, available at http://web1.millercenter.org/commissions/higher-ed/2015 -higherEdFunding-Moodys.pdf.

lower rate of enrollment growth of about 1.5 percent per year, reducing modestly the pressure of growing student numbers on per-student state spending.[9]

> 2. What are the prospects of the states' going beyond simply recovering lost ground and substantially expanding their funding efforts, as many commentators urge? Unlike the federal government, most states are not able to run budget deficits, so even in the near term, expanding state funding efforts will require either raising taxes or reallocating spending.

Given the somewhat discouraging prospect of even recovering the funding levels for higher education of the recent past, it is a challenge to picture an expansion of state funding. In some states there is clearly a strong ideological or political commitment to defunding public higher education—as typified by Governor Scott Walker's assault on the University of Wisconsin. But in that state, at least, vigorous efforts by Chancellor Rebecca Blank have given advocates of strong public universities renewed reasons for optimism.[10] Still, there is no denying that recent de-

[9] William J. Hussar and Tabitha M. Bailey, *Projections of Education Statistics to 2022* (Washington, DC: NCES, 2014), available at http://nces.ed.gov/pubs2014/2014051 .pdf, table 21.

[10] See David J. Vanness, "The Withering of a Once-Great State University," *Chronicle of Higher Education*, July 13, 2015, available at http://chronicle.com/article/The-Withering-of-a-Once-Great/231565/. See also Colleen Flaherty, "Hope in Wisconsin," *Inside Higher Ed*, September 8, 2015, available at www.insidehighered.com/news/2015/09/08/faculty-members-think-massive-donation-will-help-retain-top -professors-u-wisconsin. See Eric Kelderman, "Politics, and the Ouster of a Popular President, Cloud UNC's Search for a New Leader," *Chronicle of Higher Education*, June 11, 2015, available at http://chronicle.com/article/Politicsthe-Ouster-of-a/230825/, and "Where Scott Walker Got His Utilitarian View of Higher Education— and Why It Matters," *Chronicle of Higher Education*, September 2, 2015, available at http://chronicle.com/article/Where-Scott-Walker-Got-His/232803/.

clines in funding of public higher education have been widespread across states; although we expect to see some level of
recovery as economic prospects continue to improve, there do
not seem to be states that are generating their own push for
higher funding.

The likeliest way for substantially expanded state funding of
higher education to come about is through a system of federally
sponsored inducements or regulatory requirements. For decades,
Medicaid has been designed to reward states by providing a
positive federal match for state dollars spent on the program.[11]
Meanwhile, the existing federal student aid grant and loan arrangements may, if anything, make it easier for states to cut back
on their own commitments to funding by providing students
with other means of paying higher tuition. As some presidential
candidates have pointed out, providing substantial federal incentives to states for increasing their own commitments to higher
education may be an attractive (if potentially expensive) way to
leverage federal dollars as well to influence how states spend
their own money. Designing, let alone funding, such a program
raises many difficult challenges that we do not take up here.

3. Whatever level of funding prevails at the state level, how
   well will the states do in targeting their funds at the most
   important priorities?

If states manage to come up with additional resources, it will
be very important that those dollars be directed to achieving
major goals of the higher education system like those we have

[11] See Thomas J. Kane and Peter R. Orszag, "Funding Restrictions at Public Universities: Effects and Policy Implications," working paper, Brookings Institution, Washington, DC, 2003, available at www.brookings.edu/views/papers/orszag/20030910
.pdf.

outlined. Yet if the states *don't* come up with more money, it will become all the more important that existing resources be targeted as well as possible.

A particularly important area for state governments—and other funders of higher education as well—to focus attention on is investing in improving the effectiveness of the institutions that disadvantaged students with weak college preparation typically attend. As we have noted, one need here is to make sure students have enough financial security that they can focus on their schoolwork. But there is a good case for investing purposefully in these institutions as well. Community colleges and broad-access four-year public colleges are the least well-funded part of the higher education system, even though the students they serve face the toughest challenges for success. Work by Bound, Lovenheim, and Turner shows that cuts in per-student spending at these schools result in lower graduation rates. We also know that programs like ASAP (Accelerated Study in Associate Programs) at the City University of New York (CUNY) have raised success rates—albeit at the price of spending about 50 percent more per student than other community college programs. Moreover, we have reason to believe that investments in research about instruction for weakly prepared students—like the work at the Carnegie Foundation for the Advancement of Teaching in California and the work by TPSEMath (Transforming Post-Secondary Education in Mathematics)[12]—has the potential to pay off in greater success rates at broad-access institutions.

There is no reason to be optimistic that this effective targeting of resources will happen automatically—especially given the

[12] See the organizations' websites at www.carnegiefoundation.org/ and www.tpsemath.org/.

dubious choices some states have made in handling reductions in appropriations. There is considerable evidence, including some we have developed, that the tendency to direct subsidies toward students from families in the upper half of the income distribution does not result in greater likelihoods of enrolling in or completing college, although subsidies aimed at needier students are effective in these ways.[13] In some respects, the easiest way for states to use extra subsidy dollars is simply to cut tuition across the board, a politically popular option that may do little to advance higher education's goals.

Conclusion

Although states and the federal government should be encouraged to do what they can to ease funding pressures on both institutions and individuals, thereby promoting affordability, higher education in general should not wait for governments to solve these problems. Higher education should press ahead with other efforts to improve outcomes, including, we would hope, some we identify in this book. "Home-based" progress could in fact encourage more generous support from governments.

Payments by Individuals—and Student Aid (Including Loans)

Is Low Tuition ("Free Tuition") the Answer to Affordability?

We don't think so, largely for reasons already given in our previous discussion of the strong case for sharing the costs of higher education among various players, including both governments

---

[13] See William G. Bowen, Matthew M. Chingos, and Michael S. McPherson, *Crossing the Finish Line: Completing College at America's Public Universities* (Princeton, NJ: Princeton University Press, 2009), especially chapter 9.

and students and their families. European experience, notably in the United Kingdom, is instructive here. At one time, tuition was "free," but admission was sharply restricted to the best-prepared and generally most affluent students. Moving to a system in which students could share in the cost, partly through a loan system, enabled many more students to participate while reducing the extent of public funding of education for the most elite students.

Closer to home, the highly publicized battle at Cooper Union over charging any tuition illustrates vividly the dangers of sloganeering and insisting that "free education" is somehow sustainable or justifiable on grounds of equity. We do not summarize here the tortuous battles within and outside of the board of Cooper Union over this issue because they are described in detail in the Ithaka S+R "issue brief" referenced in the preface. Suffice it to say that the financial pressures besetting Cooper Union left it no alternative except to impose a reasonable tuition charge on those who can afford to pay—while combining such a charge with a more generous need-based financial aid program than Cooper Union could otherwise afford. There is already evidence that the initial experience with this approach has, on the merits, been successful. In fact, the ability of Cooper Union to educate at a high level the true "working poor" (who, even with free tuition, could often not afford the substantial living costs associated with going to Cooper Union, which operates in what has become a gentrified area) has been demonstrated.[14] More-

[14] In the three years just prior to charging tuition, the Pell-eligible population was around 16 percent. In the first tuition-paying class (the class that entered in Fall 2014), this number shot up to 22.5 percent. See Jamshed Bharucha, *The State of Cooper Union* (New York: Cooper Union, March 2013), available at www.support.cooper.edu/s/1289/images/editor_documents/support_cooper/thestateofcu0315.pdf.

over, it seems likely that many large, sophisticated potential donors would be reluctant to provide generous philanthropic support so that children of well-off families can get the proverbial
"free ride" as far as tuition is concerned. Many will ask, "Is this
really fair?" The answer is No![15] Finally, the ability of Cooper
Union to expand its offerings in key fields would be limited if
extra students were to impose higher costs with no tuition
offset.

There is a further point. When education is "costless" to students, they often don't finish their programs quickly. If there
are no co-payments, students don't feel as strong a need to "get
on with it" as they feel if they have to make some contribution
to the direct costs of their education. As one public university
president pointed out to us, it is no accident that at her university,

---

In the second tuition-paying class (the class entering in Fall 2015), that number
is up to 25 percent. See "Admissions Numbers Announced for 2015," Cooper Union,
news, available at http://cooper.edu/about/news/admissions-numbers-announced
-2015. There is also much other evidence that need-based aid, combined with reasonable tuition charges, increases socioeconomic diversity as compared with a
low-tuition model. For an early discussion of this broad question, see Michael S.
McPherson and Mort Schapiro, *The Student Aid Game: Meeting Need and Rewarding Talent in American Higher Education* (Princeton, NJ: Princeton University Press,
1999). In this book the authors reported a study of their own that found a statistically significant relationship for low-income students between net cost (sticker price
minus student aid) and probability of enrollment in college. They also cite an important 1995 study by Thomas Kane that looked at cross-state variations in public
college tuition—an analysis directly relevant to the Cooper Union debate. Quoting
from p. 40 of *The Student Aid Game*, Kane found that "states with high public tui-
tions have lower college-entry rates, the gap in enrollment between high- and low-
income youth is wider in high-tuition states, and within-state tuition hikes lead to
lower enrollment rates and wider gaps between high- and low-income youth."
[15] Alumni participation at Cooper Union in Fiscal Year 2014 was 22 percent—a far
cry from what many other institutions that charge tuition have achieved. See www
.cooper.edu/about/president-bharucha/archived-messages/fiscal-year-2014
-development-results.

out-of-state students generally finish their undergraduate studies in four years, while in-state students (paying appreciably lower tuition) remain in school much longer.[16]

These considerations lead us to doubt the wisdom of stating that free tuition should be even an aspirational goal (as a recent Cooper Union report urges).[17] In the innumerable disputes over the financing of higher education, it is important to keep ideology under control and to recognize that, as economists like to say, "there is no free lunch."

One has to recognize, however, that right now there is a preoccupation in political and policy circles with making at least parts of higher education "free" in one form or another for ever larger shares of the population.[18] This preoccupation is quite understandable, given the rates of increase in tuition over the past decade and more (especially at public institutions). However, we believe that moving too fast or too far in the direction of spending tax-generated dollars on relief for middle- and upper-middle income families would be a real misfortune. Moving to lower the payment burden on these families is essentially a matter of cost-shifting rather than cost reduction or cost management. It does not in itself make college more effective or more affordable for the country at large. There is little reason to

[16] We also found evidence supporting this proposition in *Crossing the Finish Line*.

[17] See "A.G. Schneiderman Announces Comprehensive Reform Package to Resolve Cooper Union Investigation and Lawsuit," press release, New York State government, September 2, 2015, available at www.ag.ny.gov/press-release/ag-schneiderman-announces-comprehensive-reform-package-resolve-cooper-union.

[18] Most recently, there has been an announcement of a new effort by President Obama and others to support free access to community colleges and to encourage grass-roots efforts along the same (and related) lines. See Goldie Blumenstyk, "President Obama to Announce a New 'College Promise' Campaign," *Chronicle of Higher Education*, September 9, 2015, available at http://chronicle.com/blogs/ticker/president-obama-to-announce-a-new-college-promise-campaign/104269.

think that lowering the payment burden on typical middle- and upper-middle-income students will cause more of them to enroll or complete college; the more serious problems with paying for college continue to lie with the problems facing disadvantaged populations. In today's environment, making large sectors of college free would confer enormous benefits on the better-off members of society and far fewer benefits on the disadvantaged, a significant number of whom do not enroll in any form of postsecondary education—never mind complete their studies if they do enroll.

Making community colleges free has fewer disadvantages because not that many well-off people attend them. However, the idea of elevating attendance at a community college to "the ideal" for those who cannot or prefer not to pay any tuition raises serious worries of other kinds. As we have seen, there is evidence that a good many community colleges are not the best starting places for students who plan to pursue a bachelor's degree. Community colleges also differ substantially in quality. Setting up an arbitrary price differential between, say, community colleges and the first two years at local four-year colleges distorts students' view of their options in unproductive ways.

Financial Aid Policies: Need-Based Aid and Merit Aid

Going back to the colonial era, and continuing through the years up until World War II, efforts were of course made to assist students of modest means to attend college. During much of that time, and certainly after passage of the Morrill Act of 1862, which provided states with grants of public land to establish colleges for the common people, the idea was that states would subsidize public university tuition sufficiently that most families from traditional college-going populations could afford to pay the costs of attending college. Meanwhile, endowments and private donations enabled private universities to finance the education of students from distinctive populations like religious denominations as well as exceptionally talented young people who would qualify for private scholarships. The students who were left out in this framework were those from low-income families with modest high school credentials and no special claim on private funding. Making college a real option for those students was a new idea for most people in the 1960s, an idea that Martin Trow described under the rubric of going "from elite to mass higher education."[19] It was an idea impelled by the more ambitious conception of equal opportunity that the War on Poverty and Great Society initiatives advanced in the 1960s and, just as important, by the emergence of a "knowledge economy" that demanded growing numbers of college-educated workers.

The first key element in the federal strategy for overcoming families' difficulties in paying for college was the provision of grants, now called Pell Grants, which low-income students can use to pay for both tuition and living expenses.[20] The focus of this program has been squarely on need since its inception, and it continues to this day to be a bedrock form of support for many students from poor families. Pell Grants targeted this population of "new" college candidates by relentlessly focusing on ability to pay as the primary criterion for support—a kind of targeting in which states had shown little interest, preferring instead to promote equity by keeping tuition low across the board. Meritorious as this program continues to be, it has defects that

[19] Martin Trow, "Problems in the Transition from Elite to Mass Higher Education," Carnegie Commission on Higher Education, Berkeley, CA, 1973.
[20] These grants were originally called Basic Education Opportunity Grants (BEOGs) and were renamed for Senator Claiborne Pell in 1980.

should be corrected, in spite of reluctance by legislators to tinker with an overwhelmingly popular program that nearly everyone acknowledges should continue to play a vital role in promoting access to post-secondary education.[21]

The second key aspect of the federal role in promoting a need-based approach was the provision of broad access to credit for students on terms that are more favorable than they could get in the private loan market through the Guaranteed Student Loan (GSL) program. This program, too, offers opportunities for improvement, but it is also, like the Pell Grant program, a fundamentally sound approach.[22]

Although the federal programs are the bedrock of national student aid approaches, accounting for almost 67 percent of all student aid in 2014–15,[23] states and individual institutions today complement the federal programs (as the federal programs once complemented them) by providing mixtures of aid based on need and aid aimed at meeting other criteria—sometimes, as in the case of many "discount" plans, intended simply to lower tuition for large groups of students. Other times, aid is targeted more narrowly based on one or another definition of "merit"— which is not to say that students who receive need-based aid lack merit. This mix of approaches is certainly understandable, given

---

[21] For example, the line between "poor" and "near-poor" candidates for assistance is too sharply drawn. Also, we have learned that simply encouraging access to college is not sufficient—more attention must be paid to ways of encouraging students to finish their studies.

[22] Originally, the GSL program relied on banks to generate loans that were then guaranteed against default by the government; later the government took over lending directly in what is now called the Direct Lending program.

[23] See College Board, *Trends in Student Aid 2015* (New York), p. 12, table 1A. In the wake of the long wars in Iraq and Afghanistan, the Post-9/11 GI Bill has also become a major source of federal student aid grant funding, amounting in 2014–15 to $13.6 billion, compared to $30.3 billion in Pell Grant funding.

the various objectives of different states and different educational institutions, but we think that a determined effort should be made to reduce the fraction of aid awarded apart from need.[24]

Merit aid in its targeted form often serves mainly to redistribute students from one college or university to another without having a great deal of effect on overall enrollment rates. Most students who qualify for special scholarships would almost certainly go to some other institution without such inducements—perhaps even to institutions better suited to their educational needs. Need-based aid, on the other hand, can have discernible effects on the enrollment of less privileged students, on where they are able to study, and on their ability to complete their studies in a timely way. There is no need to belabor these obvious points.

Groups of similar private colleges (and sometimes public ones, too) frequently find themselves in a bidding war over the same students. These bidding wars are often egged on by "enrollment management consultants" who predict dire consequences from any attempt to back down from awarding merit aid. These consultants sometimes advise multiple colleges that are competing against one another, and often intimidate local decision-makers with impenetrable mathematical models whose details are proprietary. We suspect that these consultants have been a factor causing many colleges to exaggerate the power of merit aid to solve their enrollment problems. Recent decisions by some well-known colleges to step off the merit aid escalator have yielded

---

[24] See NCES, "Trends in Undergraduate Nonfederal Grant and Scholarship Aid by Demographic and Enrollment Characteristics, Selected Years 1999–2000 to 2011–2012," NCES 2015-604, Washington, DC, September 2015, available at http://nces .ed.gov/pubs2015/2015604.pdf. College Board, *Trends in Student Aid 2014* (New York), reports that until 1981 all state-based grant aid was need-based; in recent years, about 25 percent or more of such aid has been non-need-based.

promising results. Franklin and Marshall College in Pennsylvania is a prominent example. They decided several years ago to cut back substantially on merit scholarships. They have maintained their high admissions standards, shifting aid resources from merit awards to more generous awards to high-quality students with need—investments financed in part by students from well-off families who are now paying full ("sticker") price.

Regrettably, merit aid wars are increasingly prevalent at flagship public universities as well as at private institutions. The University of Wisconsin at Madison, for example, has announced that it will provide more merit aid to in-state and out-of-state students to keep up with the competition. Chancellor Rebecca Blank has been refreshingly candid in calling this policy, from a national perspective, a "real waste." But she adds that Wisconsin can't be one of the only universities not deeply engaged in "the merit aid game." One experienced commentator (Justin Draeger, president of the National Association of Student Financial Aid Administrators) observes that: "Public universities have an increased pressure to start acting like private schools . . . You need all of the four-year schools to band together and not play the game, and I just don't know how you would get to that." He called Wisconsin's foray deeper into merit aid part of a "terrible spiral."[25]

Unfortunately, current rating systems for colleges such as the *US News* survey put real pressure on institutions to keep their average SAT scores high, even if this means "buying" students with high test scores and, in some cases, denying admission to

---

[25] Kellie Woodhouse, "Playing the Aid Game," *Inside Higher Ed*, December 18, 2015, available at https://www.insidehighered.com/news/2015/12/18/university-wisconsin-ups-its-merit-aid-effort-better-compete-peers. This article contains much useful data on practices at many flagships as well as commentary from those for and against merit aid.

high-potential students from lower-income families who simply do not test well. There are problems with this approach. In addition to considerations of equity, there is abundant evidence that grades in secondary schools are a far, far stronger predictor of success in college than are SAT scores; this is hardly surprising when we recognize that actual performance in school reflects valuable coping skills like "grit" and perseverance as well as cognitive ability.[26] It is at least moderately encouraging to note that the College Board is putting more and more emphasis on achievement tests, which are also better predictors of subsequent educational outcomes than so-called "aptitude tests" such as the SAT. Still, the rating systems take a toll, and it would be nice to see some kind of concerted action to reduce pernicious incentive and behavioral effects. It may also be possible for governments, in providing aid to institutions, to reward those that place a heavy emphasis on need-based aid.

There is, without doubt, a need to provide key kinds of information (concerning costs, financial aid, and expected outcomes, such as graduation rates) to prospective students in consistent formats while recognizing that different students will properly weight one or more variable differently. This entire set of issues clearly deserves a place on any agenda for change.

Is "Debt-Free" Education the Answer?

For reasons explained in the discussion of affordability in part II, we regard this approach as overly simplistic and certainly not "the answer" to the challenge of making college affordable for

---

[26] See Bowen, Chingos, and McPherson, *Crossing the Finish Line*, chapter 6. See also Angela L. Duckworth, Christopher Peterson, Michael D. Matthews, and Dennis R. Kelly, "Grit: Perseverance and Passion for Long-Term Goals," *Journal of Personality and Social Psychology* 92, no. 6 (2007): 1087–1101.

students in general. In the spirit of "sharing the burden," there seems no reason, as a general principle, not to expect students with good earnings prospects to be willing to "pay back" at least a modest part of the costs incurred by taxpayers and others in educating them. Resources saved in this way could then be put to more productive uses. Also, in spite of the hoopla over outlier cases in which students have clearly borrowed too much money unwisely, there is evidence that some students do not borrow enough—instead substituting too much work, often unrelated to their educational goals, to pay the costs of getting a degree in a timely way. Taking a long time to complete one's education, or never completing degree programs at all, are far larger impediments to lifetime success than incurring manageable amounts of debt—as, in fact, most borrowers do today.[27]

Federal student loan programs have, overall, played a mostly constructive role in this area, both by providing broader access to loan finance and by allowing interest rates to stay at reasonable levels. Low-cost loans, which in the early days were restricted to students of limited means, expanded opportunity by allowing disadvantaged students who lacked alternative financing to defer some of the costs of college to the future, when they could expect to be better able to pay. In particular, federally backed loans let students from disadvantaged families who lacked the resources to pay private college tuition consider a wider range of college options than they otherwise could. For many higher education analysts the mantra of the day in the 1970s and 1980s was "Pell for access; loans for choice."

---

[27] The average student debt of a bachelor's degree recipient who borrows—roughly 30 percent don't borrow at all—is around $30,000, roughly equivalent to the average cost of a new car loan.

The loan programs, however, have had some unintended and unwelcome consequences that need to be addressed. The most striking of these unexpected developments has been the emergence of the for-profit higher education industry. Before the introduction of federal student aid grants and loans, for-profit colleges were little more than a rounding error in national enrollment counts. Not so in recent years. In 2010 they accounted for 10 percent of total enrollment before declining to about 8 percent today. More than 80 percent of the revenues at student aid–eligible for-profit colleges derive from federal sources, and these colleges generated 44 percent of federal student loan defaults in the most recent data.[28] Creating a system in which colleges can compete for students in an information-poor environment with virtually all the upfront costs of attendance borne by the federal government is a recipe for trouble, and trouble there has been. We regard as promising emerging efforts to devise systems that would require institutions to share the risks of defaults by their former students.[29]

A second unanticipated consequence was the emergence of a private market for student loans that lacked the various protections and relatively low interest rates provided by federally

---

[28] To be sure, there are many for-profit colleges that manage their affairs responsibly and do important educational work. See David J. Deming, Claudia Goldin, and Lawrence F. Katz, "The For-Profit Postsecondary School Sector: Nimble Critters or Agile Predators?" *Journal of Economic Perspectives* 26, no. 1 (Winter 2012): 139–64. See also James E. Rosenbaum and Janet Rosenbaum, "Beyond BA Blinders: Lessons from Occupational Colleges and Certificate Programs for Nontraditional Students," *Journal of Economic Perspectives* 27, no. 2 (Spring 2013): 153–72.

[29] See, for example, Michael Stratford, "Lumina-Funded Paper Proposes Federal 'Risk-Sharing' Accountability System," *Inside Higher Ed*, September 9, 2015. As this article explains, this is also complicated territory, in part because of differences in loan programs and in groups of individuals who default. We don't want to create a system that "creams" the obvious winners and excludes the riskier bets.

backed loans—a development that paralleled developments in the housing market, including loosened underwriting standards and an active secondary market in packaging loans. Many students were confused by the difference between federal and private loans, sometimes borrowing privately even before exhausting their eligibility for more attractive federal loans. The use of private lending fell back after the 2008 financial crisis and now involves as few as 6 percent of borrowers, but it remains a source of some of the more extreme problems in the student loan market.[30]

There is another, widely discussed, problem associated with student loans that was only partially anticipated—the inability of some borrowers to repay without seriously damaging their life chances. The main factors that explain these cases include failure to complete programs, enrolling at for-profit colleges that rely heavily on student borrowing even for high-risk, low-pay-off programs, taking on private debt, and making highly imprudent educational plans. These problems need to be addressed, but they have little to do with the ubiquitous reference to $1.2 trillion of debt or with the experience of typical college graduates.[31]

---

[30] See Tara Siegel Bernard, "The Many Pitfalls of Private Student Loans," *New York Times*, September 4, 2015, available at www.nytimes.com/2015/09/05/your-money/student-loans/the-many-pitfalls-of-private-student-loans.html?_r=0. Private student loans offer lenders an advantage they can't get from other unsecured personal loans: a special rule that makes it very difficult to declare bankruptcy. There is little rationale for affording lenders this special protection, and indeed there is, in our view, no good reason why the law should recognize a distinct category of "private student loans" distinct from other unsecured debt. Eliminating that category would solve the bankruptcy problem for these private loans but would also avoid the continuing risk that students and families become confused between these different categories of loans while still allowing banks to issue unsecured loans to students if they chose to do so.

[31] Since 2007 borrowers in good standing have had access to a federal income-contingent repayment program. This program limits obligations to repay to a fraction of one's income and has proved to be a helpful safety net for some students. But

These focused problems require focused solutions—not a generalized judgment that borrowing is inherently evil.

Some of the most fundamental challenges facing the federal student aid system at this juncture arise less from unanticipated consequences than from features of the programs that are intrinsic to their original design. Among the problems of the core federal grant and loan programs are (1) their failure to encourage timely college completion, (2) their more general absence of accountability for results, and (3) their continuing tendency to extend their mission as new constituencies have arisen. None of these difficulties was evident or urgent in the early days of these programs. However, the vast expansion of the federal role and the relative shrinkage of state funding has made addressing these

---

no one can claim that this program is free from problems. There is the generic problem of adverse selection, which has been discussed ever since Jim Tobin and Kingman Brewster at Yale introduced this idea decades ago. Also, there are cases of outlier borrowers. There are very rare but highly publicized stories of people who have gotten in trouble by borrowing over $100,000 with little to show for it; these almost always involve either piling private borrowing on top of federal loans or enrolling in graduate programs with little employment potential. This has not been a serious problem with undergraduate borrowing because there is a ceiling on the total lifetime federal debt one can take on for undergraduate study. But there is no longer any limit on the amount of money graduate students can borrow (except that in any given year students cannot borrow more than the full cost of attendance less other aid). People enrolling in multiple master's programs or in very long-term programs could easily amass debt they will never be able to repay. It is obvious that a program designed this way creates a standing temptation for expensive graduate programs to raise their tuition. As Sandy Baum has said, "What we're doing is randomly subsidizing lots of people without careful thought" ("Grad-School Loan Binge Fans Debt Worries," *Wall Street Journal,* August 18, 2015). This debt would then all be forgiven by the federal government, and the resulting losses on the federal books could result in a major backlash against what is at base a valuable program. (See Jason DeLisle and Alexander Holt, "Zero Marginal Cost: Measuring Subsidies for Graduate Education in the Public Service Loan Forgiveness Program," New America Foundation, Washington, DC, September 2014, available at www.edcentral.org/wp-content/up loads/2014/09/ZeroMarginalCost_140910_DelisleHolt.pdf.)

challenges an important and urgent part of the agenda for improvement of American higher education.

An Over-Arching Question: How to Advance the Evolving Federal Role

We do not have space here to discuss in any detail the broader questions, some philosophical, that are endemic in thinking more broadly about how the federal role in supporting students should evolve. But we do want to at least identify some issues and opportunities. We should not forget that the federal government did not begin contributing regularly to college finance in peacetime until the late 1960s, entering a field where state governments (and local ones to a much smaller extent) were the dominant players.[32] When federal leaders did step in, they did so quite explicitly under the banner of equal opportunity, as part of Lyndon B. Johnson's Great Society initiative. From the beginning, the federal government, in an act of self-conscious deference to the states and the private colleges, avoided directly funding or asserting authority over the operations of colleges and universities.

A largely unstated assumption was that if the financial barriers to entering college were reduced, the actual experience of college for disadvantaged students would look much like that of their wealthier peers and that students from poor families would enjoy comparable completion rates and later life success. The problem was conceived to be that of providing access, not that of promoting success. A second untested assumption was that families would generally do a good job in selecting which

---

[32] This is not to overlook the fact that the federal government made huge contributions through the Morrill Acts of 1862 and 1890, which provided grants of land for the construction of colleges, and also invested substantially in supporting the education of veterans following World War II and other wars since then.

college students should attend. Both of these assumptions have proved problematic.

None of the federal programs was designed with the aim of giving the federal government significant capacity to influence the *performance* of colleges and universities in contrast to who gets the opportunity to attend them. Some architects of the federal aid system, who were sympathetic to a market-oriented approach to social investment, might have said, or might say now, that competition will take care of the quality problem. Both Pell Grants and the loan system in essence provide vouchers, and they invite reliance on informed consumers to identify quality and to vote for it with their feet.

While this point of view has its place, both reflection and forty years of experience reveal its limits. This is a market in which information is hard to find and hard to trust. It is a market most people enter only a few times in their lifetimes, so experience is not a good teacher—and there is no easy way for individuals on their own to judge the quality of an educational program without experiencing it. We have plenty of evidence of poor decision-making in the face of these obstacles to the working of an ideal marketplace. Some for-profit colleges and some private loan programs show that poor information can be exploited, especially when directed at those who have little experience of how college education works. The horror stories that regularly appear in newspapers recounting terribly foolish college choices that result in awful outcomes provide further evidence. As economist Arthur Okun said many years ago, "The market has its place, but must be kept in its place." Given how important federal voucher-type spending has become in shaping the market for higher education, it is no longer plausible (if it ever was) that simply handing out the money and letting the market do its work is an adequate conception of the federal role.

The main lesson we want to draw, then, is that if more federal resources are going to be devoted to the finance of undergraduate education, whether through "taxing the rich" or otherwise, they should be spent purposefully to advance the larger goals of public investments in higher education. Almost the entire federal effort in college finance has been organized around the "access" problem: putting dollars, whether granted or loaned, in people's hands to help them attend college. This has been a powerful tool in giving Americans, especially disadvantaged Americans, the opportunity to begin college. No doubt the access problem is still not fully solved, but the bigger problems we now face include timely college success and cost management (a prerequisite to resolving the nation's college affordability problem). While spending more money may well be a necessary part of addressing such problems, simply sending people checks—which is what the federal aid system is designed to do—is unlikely to do the job.

Taking an active role in shaping the performance of colleges and universities is new and difficult territory for the Department of Education to enter into, and it needs to be explored with caution and humility. In recent years, the government has taken small steps in this direction, for example, by reducing the number of years of full-time study for which a student can receive a Pell Grant from nine to six.[33] But at times the department has overreached. For example, setting out to rate the performance of every college and university in the United States—an effort

---

[33] See https://studentaid.ed.gov/sa/types/grants-scholarships/pell/calculate-eligibility.

that has now been put aside—was an implausibly ambitious early step. More generally, we have to recognize that a more activist federal role carries with it real dangers of foolish (and costly) forms of regulation—and, simply, of over-regulation.

If the Department of Education does elect to move more aggressively into this new territory, we have some general guidelines to suggest:

1. Develop programs that fund states or institutions directly, and key the funding to measurable performance. A simple example is rewarding institutions with federal dollars for their success in advancing low-income students toward graduation. It is one thing to reward institutions for getting low-income students to enroll; it is another thing to reward institutions for getting Pell Grant students to succeed, which the existing Pell Grant program does not do.

2. Strive to make the federal government a partner in state and institutional efforts rather than a substitute for them. Matching grants can be a useful tool.

3. Create a stronger federal presence in providing information and counseling to students about college choice, program choice, and financing options.

4. Invest systematically in developing higher-quality data, and promote greater transparency in reporting on finances, operations, and outcomes.

5. Invest in well-designed experiments and other types of research intended to test innovations at both institutional and state levels.

6. Invest in the Department of Education's own capacity to work actively with states and institutions on measuring

their performance and improving their work. It is striking that there is less than one Department of Education
employee for every college and university in the United
States.[34] Such leanness is admirable in some respects, but
it reflects the fact that the department is designed, at both
the K–12 and higher-education levels, to be principally a
check-writing organization.

If the federal commitment to college finance extends from
passive check-writing to more active attempts to promote demanding goals like college completion and greater accountability, it is vital that the goal of reducing inequities, not only in
college access but also in college success, remain central. Reducing inequities is, to be sure, far from an easy challenge to meet.
Disadvantaged students are more likely than others to enroll in
degree and certificate programs in which their chances of success are quite low and there is a real risk that students emerging
from such programs, having borrowed for programs that didn't
help them, will actually be made worse off by their encounter
with college. This is an area ripe for experimentation, and an
area in which there are signs of valuable learning about how to
build more effective programs.[35] This is also an area where effective college guidance is sorely needed and difficult to come by.
All these areas are excellent candidates for federal–state partnerships and, in the important area of vocational preparation, for
partnerships with business. Focused attention on these problems
is likely to depend, in many states, on federal leadership, and

[34] Education is by far the smallest department in the federal government, as measured by personnel.
[35] See City University of New York (CUNY), Accelerated Study in Associate Programs, at www1.cuny.edu/sites/asap/.

those efforts depend on the federal government's recognizing that improving the educational prospects of disadvantaged students is at the core of its mission.

Increasing Efficiency

Who could be against increasing the "efficiency" with which higher education is delivered? Surely no one, provided that "efficiency" is properly understood to encompass not just the direct costs of higher education but the outcomes achieved along the way. "Cheaper" is not necessarily "better," but it can be. A major barrier to clear thinking in this area is the difficulty of agreeing on how various outcomes are to be valued. We take the simplified approach of identifying as desirable outcomes the measurable metrics discussed in part II: greater educational attainment overall, higher age-specific completion rates, shorter time-to-degree, and reduction in disparities in outcomes related to race or ethnicity and SES—all seen in relation to the cost of producing the outcomes in question. Deeper measures of outcomes such as enhanced creativity, improved critical thinking, better social skills, and civic contributions are too complex for this short book and for the state of existing measurement capabilities—though they are hardly unimportant.

Is "Administrative Bloat" a Big Problem?

As we saw in part II, the principal explanation for the rapid rise in tuition prices in public higher education over the past decade has been the decline in state government funding per student. Some observers are skeptical of that explanation, viewing it as too convenient a way for campus leaders to let themselves off the hook. In response, these observers have tried to advance explanations that would say costs are going up because of irresponsible increases in spending, notably on administration (superfluous deans and administrators, excessive provision of "services," and so on). There is, however, a different set of questions concerning college cost that requires investigation. Even if the rise in tuition is not an indication that public colleges and universities are becoming more wasteful and thereby causing price hikes, it's still fair to ask if there are ways to reduce costs in public higher education without accompanying declines in quality. That is, even if rising college costs didn't cause the tuition increases, reductions in college costs could help to slow increases or, in the best case, reverse them.

But before we take up the question of what smart reductions in spending colleges might do well to undertake, we must first clear away the distracting but ultimately unconvincing claim that a ballooning of the number of administrators in colleges— so-called administrative bloat—is what lies behind the rapid growth in public college tuition. We should note first that there simply has not been a rapid increase in per-student expenditures in public higher education that needs to be explained. Between academic years 2001–02 and 2011–12, average expenditures per student in public doctoral universities grew by less than 1 percent per year above inflation, and the same was true in master's- and bachelor's-level public institutions. At community colleges, spending per student actually failed to keep up with inflation over that decade. Meanwhile, published tuition prices were rising at much higher rates. It's just not true that rapid expenditure growth drove tuition increases.

The question remains: How can we get those facts to jibe with claims like that of Paul Campos in the *New York Times* that "administrative positions at colleges and universities grew by

60 percent between 1993 and 2009?"[36] That certainly sounds like a major cost driver. First, however, it helps to notice that between 1993 and 2009 enrollment in colleges and universities grew by 42 percent.[37] Thus these "administrative positions" (probably mislabeled, in part, as we explain later) were at best actually growing at about 1 percent per year on a per-student basis over that period. Second, it's not clear just how Campos and others who make this argument are defining administrative positions. Properly understanding the shifts over time in personnel in higher education requires a closer look at just where the growth has been. In table 4, which is based on government statistics, we get a richer picture of the evolution of non-faculty staffing in public higher education. We can see that the ratio of "executive, administrative, and managerial staff" to students actually fell slightly over the twenty years from 1991 to 2011, from 1.1 administrators per 100 FTE students to 1.0 to 100.

Growth has occurred among professional staff *outside* the administrative staff, a group that went from 3.4 professionals per 100 in 1991 to 4.3 per 100 in 2011. Meanwhile, reliance on non-professional staff has fallen by about a third as a ratio of staff to students. What is actually going on is shrinkage per student in the non-professional (low-skill) workforce, who are being replaced by professionals. This phenomenon echoes developments in the economy as a whole.[38] As technology advances, relatively low-

---

[36] See Paul F. Campos, "The Real Reason College Tuition Costs So Much," *New York Times*, April 4, 2015, available at www.nytimes.com/2015/04/05/opinion/sunday/the-real-reason-college-tuition-costs-so-much.html?_r=0.

[37] NCES, "Digest of Education Statistics, Tables, and Figures," Washington, DC, 2014, available at https://nces.ed.gov/programs/digest/d14/tables/dt14_303.10.asp?current=yes.

[38] See David Autor, "Skills, Education, and the Rise of Earnings Inequality among the 'Other 99 Percent,'" *Science*, May 23, 2014.

TABLE 4. Full-Time-Equivalent (FTE) Staff in Public Colleges and
Universities per 100 FTE Students, by Category and Year, 1991, 2001,
2011

Staff Category	Year and Number per 100		
	1991	2001	2011
Faculty	5.7	6.2	5.9
Graduate Assistants	0.9	1.0	1.1
Executive/Administrative/Managerial	1.1	0.9	1.0
Other Professionals	3.4	4.3	4.3
Non-professional Staff	7.4	6.7	5.0
TOTAL	18.4	19.2	17.3

Source: National Center for Education Statistics, *Digest of Education Statistics*, 2012
(Washington, DC), table 285.

skilled jobs like typing, filing, and lawn-cutting get squeezed out
by greater mechanization and computerization. At the same time,
the use of new technologies increases the need for information
technology professionals, scientific support personnel, and so on.
What we are seeing is not "administrative bloat" but the profes-
sionalization of non-faculty staff. Indeed, the aggregate reliance on
non-faculty personnel in public higher education has actually
fallen modestly, from 11.9 staff per 100 students in 1991 to 10.3
staff per 100 students in 2011. Undoubtedly the growth in non-
administrative professionals relative to non-professional staff has
meant an increase in average staff salaries, but this trend is also
consistent with broader trends in the economy, and those higher
salaries probably reflect higher productivity.[39]

[39] It is disappointing to see comments by Arne Duncan, the former secretary of education, that misstate the nature of these changes and provide support for the wrong--

Thinking straight about the issue of the costs of higher education in the United States requires putting aside the tempting but unsupportable claim that tuition at public universities has grown because of an explosion of wasteful expenditures on college administration. Instead, we must think harder about where to find the real inefficiencies—and the real opportunities for cost savings and productivity growth.

How Many PhD Programs—and of What Kinds—Does the Nation Really Need?

The greatest single opportunity to reduce costs and inefficiencies in the university sector lies in rationalizing PhD programs. As early as the 1970s, Allan M. Cartter warned that there would be a serious oversupply of PhDs in the 1970s. But no one paid much, if any, attention to his analysis.[40] Subsequently, Bowen and Rudenstine provided a wealth of detail concerning trends in PhD programs and doctorates in six major fields through 1988; they found rapid increases in the number of PhD programs, especially in small and lower-rated programs—in spite of a marked slow-down in the number of openings for new tenure-track faculty.[41]

---

headed notion that "administrative bloat" is a big problem. See Albert H. Hunt, "Arne Duncan, Education Secretary, Sees Challenges for U.S. Colleges," *New York Times*, November 8, 2015.

[40] Allan M. Cartter, "The Academic Labor Market," in *Higher Education and the Labor Market* (New York: McGraw Hill, 1974), pp. 281–307; Carnegie Commission on Higher Education, *Ph.D.'s and the Academic Labor Market* (New York: McGraw Hill, 1976).

[41] William G. Bowen and Neil L. Rudenstine, *In Pursuit of the PhD* (Princeton, NJ: Princeton University Press, 1992), especially chapter 4. Back in 1960, Bernard Berelson anticipated these developments and described the dynamic at work in stimulating the growth of new graduate programs: "The colonization of the underdeveloped institutions by ambitious products of the developed ones who then seek to

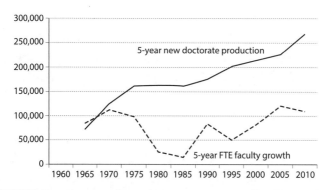

FIGURE 7: Growth in Numbers of New Doctorates and Numbers of New Full-Time-Equivalent (FTE) Faculty (Five-Year Intervals), 1965–2010
Source: National Center for Education Statistics, *Digest of Education Statistics* (Washington, DC, various years).

Michael McPherson and Charles Kurose at the Spencer Foundation have written a carefully crafted (unpublished) memo revisiting Allan Cartter's point that the level of PhD production should be expected to be a function of the rate of growth in the size of the faculty. Thus, when the rate of growth for tenure-track faculty declines, this relationship should produce a *decline* in PhD production, not just a halt to growth. But this has not been the case. McPherson and Kurose show graphically (in figure 7) that there has been a dramatic increase in PhD production relative to the growth in FTE faculty. By the mid-1980s, "growth in the number of faculty was only enough to absorb 10 to 16 percent of the PhDs produced."[42]

Leaders of higher education have not been oblivious to this worrying trend. Robert Berdahl, then president of the Associa-

---

make the colony a competitor of the mother university." See Berelson, *Graduate Education in the United States* (New York: McGraw Hill, 1960), p. 35.
[42] Michael S. McPherson and Charles Kurose, "Imbalance in Faculty Labor Markets," unpublished memo, September 23, 2014.

tion of American Universities (AAU), bravely asked in 2009 how many PhD programs the country really needs—but the study resulting from his raising this provocative question produced very little, and the problem has only grown worse since the Berdahl initiative.[43]

Established faculty and their professional associations are understandably reluctant to take on these issues, but we believe their long-run interest would be served better by addressing uncomfortable choices than by leaving it to legislatures to propose—and insist on—major changes. In May 2014, the Modern Language Association (MLA) Taskforce on Doctoral Study in Modern Literature issued a report calling for a major redesign of doctoral programs that would shorten time-to-degree, emphasize new pedagogies, and encourage new modes of scholarship.[44] There is much to admire in this report, but (not surprisingly) it rejects calls for reductions in program size and fails to consider at all the super-sensitive question of whether there are just too many programs.

Professional associations have been active in identifying jobs that humanities PhDs can fill outside the academy, an understandable response to an obvious oversupply of doctorates. It is surely correct, as the MLA recently asserted, that "having doc-

[43] See Paul Basken, "U.S. May Need to Prune Number of Research Universities, Lobby Group Says," *Chronicle of Higher Education*, June 26, 2009, available at http://chronicle.com/article/US-May-Need-to-Prune-Number/47339. See also Committee on Research Universities, Board on Higher Education and Workforce, Policy and Global Affairs, *Research Universities and the Future of America: Ten Breakthrough Actions Vital to Our Nation's Prosperity and Security* (Washington, DC: National Academies Press, 2012), available at http://sites.nationalacademies.org/pga/bhew/researchuniversities/.

[44] See Colleen Flaherty, "5-Year Plan," *Inside Higher Ed*, May 28, 2014, available at www.insidehighered.com/news/2014/05/28/mla-report-calls-phd-program-reform-including-cutting-time-degree.

toral experience may allow immediate entry to more responsible and challenging jobs than those available to someone directly out of college." After all, PhD seekers are generally highly intelligent and ambitious. But surely someone whose goal was to become a museum curator or a copyeditor at an advertising firm could have gotten there with less expense and lost time than a PhD requires. The energetic efforts of the MLA, the American Historical Association, and others to tout non-academic jobs is itself evidence of the oversupply of PhDs in these fields.

The interest of individual universities in maintaining their PhD programs is easily understood. Having these programs is a major path to status in higher education, and such programs, no doubt, make it easier to hire faculty and to convince legislatures that "University X" really is to be admired; also, PhD programs yield graduate-student research and teaching assistants who themselves contribute to both scholarly and teaching functions. A study by the Rand Corporation that has been too often overlooked points directly to the "prestige-seeking" desire of universities and to the consequences of this drive.[45]

To the best of our knowledge, there has been no good cost-simulation study of the potential cost-savings that could follow from the closing down, or at least the slimming down, of a number of the lower-ranked PhD programs. Such a study would be hard to do well because many of the potential savings are hard to quantify and would take time to capture, but it is badly needed. A major consequence should be a shift over time in the required qualifications of a number of faculty members. At

[45] See Dominic J. Brewer, Susan M. Gates, and Charles J. Goldman, *In Pursuit of Prestige: Strategy and Competition in U.S. Higher Education* (New Brunswick, NJ: Transaction Publishers, 2004). "Prestige," in turn, is clearly linked to the number and scale of PhD programs.

present, faculty at PhD-granting institutions are normally given smaller teaching loads because of the perceived need to give them the research opportunities required both to attract graduate students and to generate opportunities for professional advancement. If more faculty were hired primarily for their skills or interest in teaching, there would be less justification for subsidizing research time of uncertain value. (See our discussion in the next section of the case for a professionalized "teaching corps.") The direct costs of supporting graduate programs are also far from inconsequential. In addition, there are obvious implications for capital costs and for infrastructure costs in general. Our guess is that the potential savings that could result from scaling back PhD programs are substantial.

We do not want to be misunderstood. Our country badly needs to support PhD programs of the highest quality generously, and this implies supporting their associated research efforts. We recognize that any argument for placing even more emphasis on strengthening the leading programs while reducing the resources devoted to other programs raises all sorts of obvious political problems. Such a realignment of priorities could make it harder to achieve the diversity in faculty ranks that is needed— but this is a problem that should be attacked directly, and not through failing to address the current overproduction of PhDs in a variety of academic fields, including the sciences in some cases. A large chorus of charges of elitism would surely be heard—and, to be sure, it is a merit-based elitism in the support of PhD programs that we favor.[46]

---

[46] There are legitimate concerns that admission to the best academic graduate programs and to employment in top departments may rely too much on academic pedigree and "insider" advantages. This, too, is a problem that should be addressed directly.

Political obstacles notwithstanding, rationalizing graduate education requires some reduction in the number of programs and in enrollments at programs that continue to exist, as well as a general shortening of time-to-degree. It is far from obvious, however, how this can be accomplished. Reluctant as we are to suggest more reporting requirements, one modest step might be for a state or federal agency to require simple reports on completion rates for PhD programs, time-to-degree, and career outcomes. More transparency along these lines might help—if reporting requirements were not over-done (a real risk).

An even more fundamental question is whether PhD programs are focused on teaching the most relevant skills. Phillip A. Griffiths, a distinguished mathematician and former head of the Institute for Advanced Study, believes that in his field there continues to be too much of a tendency to prepare students for tenure-track positions that emphasize breakthrough scholarship in traditional fields of mathematics. There is obviously a shortage of attractive tenure-track positions requiring traditional forms of graduate education. In addition, there is an equally clear need to improve dramatically the teaching of undergraduate mathematics—which, as we discuss later in this book, is a major source of some of our most vexing national issues, including low completion rates and marked disparities in outcomes related to SES. In Griffith's view (expressed in a personal conversation with Bowen), it is vitally important to improve teaching talents and reinforce the notion that teaching is a noble calling.[47]

---

[47] For a broader statement of the case for shifting the emphasis in some graduate programs toward teaching, see Leonard Cassuto, "Why We Need to Remember the Doctorate-of-Arts Degree," *Chronicle of Higher Education*, September 9, 2015. See also Leonard Cassuto's book *The Graduate School Mess: What Caused It and How We*

Doctoral education in its traditional form can be said to be the most successful achievement of American universities, as recognized around the world and as evidenced by the continuing interest of many of the world's most talented students in coming to this country for advanced training. Sadly, in terms of effective use of scarce resources, parts of the graduate education establishment can also be regarded as the "soft underbelly" of American higher education. To be sure, history teaches us that raising serious questions about how many resources the country should invest in a multiplicity of PhD programs (and in PhD programs of what kind) is the proverbial "third rail" in higher education circles. Nonetheless, risky as it will be to bring off, a tough re-examination of both real national needs and costs definitely seems in order.[48]

Can Colleges and Universities Improve Their Management of Student Progress toward Degrees?

Important as it is to be aware of broad patterns (such as the clear relationship between selectivity and graduation rates, even after accounting for differences in the academic preparation and other characteristics of incoming students), it is just as impor-

---

Can Fix It (Cambridge, MA: Harvard University Press, 2015). There is also some evidence of increasing graduate student dissatisfaction with the current state of affairs (Vimal Patel, "How the U. of Missouri Became a Hotbed for Graduate Student Activism," *Chronicle of Higher Education*, September 4, 2015).

[48] This is the point of view expressed forcefully by Rob Jenkins, "Stop Resisting a 2-Tier System," *Chronicle of Higher Education*, September 28, 2015. Jenkins writes: "The truth … is that most of the college teaching jobs that exist today—at least in the humanities—do not really require a Ph.D. That is, although the job announcements might 'require' it, the job itself does not.… We have created an entire class of professionals who are essentially overqualified for most of the available positions." Jenkins advocates "a new, teaching-focused graduate degree specifically designed to prepare people for the teaching-focused jobs they might actually get."

tant to recognize that there are pronounced differences in educational outcomes among students at seemingly similar institutions.[49] Much research is needed to understand these differences and to learn lessons from the most successful "outliers" among institutions. We can do no more here than identify this set of opportunities to improve efficiency by facilitating the timely completion of degree programs. One obvious pre-requisite to success is an institution's determination to work hard on this set of problems and to enlist the active support of not only key administrators but also faculty.

Providing clear paths to graduation, and good guidance, can pay big dividends, as can hard work on ensuring access to gateway courses and success in surmounting what often seem daunting curricular barriers. We are persuaded that there are real opportunities for individual institutions, and groups of institutions, to reduce the costs per degree by working assiduously along these lines. It is striking, and encouraging, to see how many seemingly modest efforts to increase completion rates are underway. Circumstances of individual institutions vary so much that there is surely a multitude of promising paths forward, and it is important, as we said in our earlier discussion of federal and state programs, to reward instances of good work.[50] This

[49] See Frederick M. Hess, Mark Schneider, Andrew P. Kelly, and Kevin Carey, "Diplomas and Dropouts," *American Enterprise Institute*, June 3, 2009, available at www .aei.org/publication/diplomas-and-dropouts/.

[50] Valuable progress on this potpourri of issues by a wide variety of individuals deserves to be recognized. We can mention here only the 2008 menu of "high-impact" educational practices identified by the AAC&U (and George Kuh), the impressive earlier work by Vincent Tinto, and the more recent contributions of the Lumina Foundation. (For citations and more discussion, see Bowen, Chingos, and McPherson, *Crossing the Finish Line*, pp. 220ff.) Improvements aimed at degree completion at community colleges are discussed in Thomas Bailey, Shanna Smith Jaggers, and Davis Jenkins, *Redesigning America's Community Colleges: A Clearer Path to Student*

institution-specific approach to improving "efficiency," properly defined, deserves more emphasis that it is usually given.

Putting High-Profile College Sports in Proper Perspective

When we first drafted this manuscript, we put the discussion of high-profile sports under the broad heading of curbing costs. On further reflection, we think that the most insidious aspects of the growing intensity and escalating costs of high-profile sports are more indirect. The "arms race" to stay competitive—or to become competitive—is so well known that it requires no discussion here. Only a relatively small number of exceptional programs (estimated at 10 to 15 percent of Division I schools) make money for their institutions—and even in these cases, the capital costs of providing top-line facilities are not always taken into account. The pressure to spend money to excel competitively is driven in part by dreams of cracking into the truly "big time" (with associated TV revenues) and in part by what one may call quasi-jingoistic notions of achieving the alleged reputational value of competing successfully with the strongest teams in the country—even if it costs a lot of money to indulge these notions.[51]

Success (Cambridge, MA: Harvard University Press, 2015). A widely cited example of an institution employing the approach Bailey and colleagues advocate is CUNY's Accelerated Study in Associate Programs (ASAP), whose website is www1.cuny .edu/sites/asap/.

[51] See Gilbert M. Gaul, *Billion Dollar Ball: A Journey through the Big-Money Culture of College Football* (New York: Random House, 2015), reviewed by Carlos Lozada in the *Washington Post*, August 21, 2015. See also Jenny Jarvie, "University in Alabama Ends Football Program, Angering Just About Everyone," *Los Angeles Times*, December 31, 2014, available at www.latimes.com/nation/la-na-alabama-football-20141231 -story.html, and Ken Bradley, "Months after Being Killed, UAB Football Reinstated," *Sporting News*, June 1, 2015, available at www.sportingnews.com/ncaa-football/

The number of institutions where these spiraling costs have direct effects on financial well-being are, however, relatively few. The indirect effects of the widely publicized excesses in spending by some institutions are more pervasive and, to our way of thinking, more serious. Most fundamentally, they are at odds with the integrity of educational missions and undermine the confidence of many members of the public at large in the priorities of higher education, and in its capacity to enforce wise priorities. They make many institutions look reckless and wasteful. These practices also affect the morale of faculty asked to make sacrifices of their own in order to save resources—and, in the process, surely make faculty less inclined to live with hard trade-offs and to consider potentially revolutionary ways of improving teaching methods. The bullying of university presidents by powerful coaches and donors that trustees sometimes tolerate (or, worse, encourage) threatens the legitimacy of the entire university authority structure. Finally, undue emphasis on big-time sports can skew the giving patterns of consequential donors and affect the composition of boards of directors or regents.

The truly interesting question is not what drives this machine but how one might curb the ever-rising costs of big-time competition. At one point many of us thought that giving more authority to presidents was a possible answer. But it now seems clear that this is not the answer. Gilbert M. Gaul's new book, cited earlier, provides a fascinating description of the efforts to address the problem of two of the most forward-looking leaders of institutions of higher education (William "Brit" Kirwan, former chancellor of the University System of Maryland, and

---

story/2015–06–01/uab-football-reinstated-rumors-ray-watts-program-returns
-killed-birmingham.

Holden Thorp, then at the University of North Carolina and now at Washington University). Gaul's conclusion is that even courageous presidents cannot make much difference as long as the commercial and political pressures to win are so great. Boards of regents or trustees are too often unwilling to support strong actions that threaten "competitiveness."[52]

We have come, however reluctantly, to believe that the only realistic paths to saving serious amounts of money—and, even more important, restoring some semblance of integrity to college sports seen as part of an institution's educational mission—are through legal challenges to the "system" or even direct governmental action. It is conceivable that recent findings that high-profile athletes are "employees," obligated to hew to incredibly time-demanding schedules, will lead the courts to conclude that programs of this kind violate the anti-trust laws, which would presumably mean the demise of the National Collegiate Athletic Association as a rule-making authority.[53] This could, in turn, undermine the willingness of some universities to spend ever-increasing amounts of money on paying players, raising coaches' salaries, and the like; there could be a bifurcation between universities willing to spend whatever it takes to field the best teams in the country and others reluctant to see even greater divides in the treatment afforded recruited athletes versus students at large.[54]

[52] Ibid.

[53] The National Labor Relations Board (NLRB) ruling that Northwestern athletes cannot unionize does not affect this line of argument. The ruling did not address the finding that these athletes are "employees." See Eric Kelderman, "NLRB's Northwestern Ruling Sets a High Bar for Approving Student-Athlete Unions," *Chronicle of Higher Education*, August 18, 2015, available at http://chronicle.com/article/NLRB-s-Northwestern-Ruling/232441/.

[54] A most interesting (and encouraging) interview with Father John I. Jenkins, president of Notre Dame, suggests that even football powers like Notre Dame might be unwilling to pay athletes in a newly competitive environment. (Dan Berry, "Notre

But this could be wishful thinking. A recent article on the football program of the University of Alabama extols the financial gains to the institution overall, as well as to its athletic program, of winning big-time.[55] However accurate or inaccurate the figures cited in this story (and we have no way of checking them), our worry is that this tale of alleged great "success" will encourage any number of other programs, of varying degrees of athletic quality, to believe that they can "become Alabama." "Wannabes" are everywhere.

We cannot judge how these developments will play out; we can do no more here than identify what is an obvious, and embarrassing, problem for higher education. It is more than mildly ironic that the regents of the University of Illinois, for example, are vocally distressed by retention bonuses in the hundreds of thousands dollars owed to the leaders of their system but seemingly indifferent to, or supportive of, multi-million-dollar salaries for top coaches (and now assistant coaches) that make the compensation of chancellors and presidents seem puny in comparison.[56]

Rationalizing Staffing: Supporting the Development of a "Teaching Corps"

There has been a dramatic shift in the mix of faculty—from tenure-track to "conditional," "adjunct," or whatever word one wants to use to describe the variety of teaching staff that comprise

---

Dame Stands Firm Amid Shifts in College Athletics," *New York Times*, September 10, 2015). Henry S. Bienen, former president of Northwestern, espouses essentially the same point of view (see Bienen, "Private Colleges Wouldn't Pay for Play").

[55] See Joe Drape, "Alabama Is Rolling in Cash, with Tide Lifting All Boats," *New York Times*, November 5, 2015, available at www.nytimes.com/2015/11/07/sports/ncaa football/alabama-crimson-tide-football-marketing.html?_r=0.

[56] See Jack Stripling, "Stage Is Set for Uncommon Ugliness in Illinois Chancellor's Exit," *Chronicle of Higher Education*, August 13, 2015.

the non-tenure-track (NTT) faculty. In 1969, tenured and tenure-track faculty accounted for over three quarters of all faculty; in 2009, tenured and tenure-track faculty accounted for just one-third of all faculty.[57] This shift is, we believe, irreversible. It is the product of two forces. First, on the demand side of the equation, many institutions have felt the need to curb increases in staffing costs, and NTT faculty are of course much less expensive than tenure-track faculty: they are less well paid, they are asked to teach more hours, their performance can be assessed with less controversy than the performance of tenure-track faculty, and they can be released if need be.[58] A certain amount of attention to scholarship can be justified for all teaching staff as a form of professional development, but it need not be either expensive or extensive. Second, on the supply side, the large number of aspiring faculty who cannot find tenure-track positions (discussed earlier) has provided a pool of potential teachers, many of whom prefer NTT positions to no spot in academia at all.

It does no good to bemoan this shift, as a number of people insist on doing.[59] The underlying market forces are not to be

[57] See William G. Bowen and Eugene M. Tobin, *Locus of Authority: The Evolution of Faculty Roles in the Governance of Higher Education* (Princeton, NJ: Princeton University Press, 2015), pp. 152ff., for documentation of this shift and a fuller discussion of the reasons for it.

[58] Much anecdotal evidence teaches us that in some limited number of situations (by no means all), faculty with tenure do not, in fact, either produce research of consequence or teach well; post-tenure review processes often need to be strengthened. Another factor, still in its early stages, is the "unbundling" of some teaching functions as a result of technological advances. "Unbundling" reduces the need for faculty to manage all aspects of a course. See William G. Bowen, "Academia Online: Musings (Some Unconventional)," Stafford Little Lecture, Princeton University, Princeton, NJ, October 14, 2013.

[59] See, for example, the proposal by Democratic presidential candidate Bernie Sanders to require institutions to retain a certain ratio of tenured to NTT faculty—an idea that ignores entirely the realities of the situation. According to Sanders, "States

denied, and people should recognize candidly that the use of NTT faculty is often justified. There are, to be sure, pronounced differences in the case for using NTT faculty in some institutions and some settings as opposed to others. The wealthiest, most selective, most privileged schools will continue to make only limited use of this set of people, whereas the far larger number of mainstream public and private schools will make more use of them. We should simply accept this situation as reality. Each institution has to do what it can afford and what is consistent with its sense of its own character and mission.

Rather than yearn for a return to an alleged "Golden Age" that is not sustainable, it is far wiser for higher education to make the best accommodation it can to the shift in faculty mix that has transpired and find ways to make effective use of the still-growing ranks of NTT faculty. This topic ranks high on our agenda of opportunities both to do better in terms of educational outcomes and to control costs.

There is growing evidence that NTT faculty, when properly chosen, supported, and treated, can be highly effective teachers, especially of basic, "foundational" courses. Perhaps the best-known study to reach this conclusion is the one by David Figlio, Morton O. Schapiro, and Kevin B. Soter at Northwestern.[60] Putting aside any general presumption that tenure-track faculty

---

would have to promise that, within five years, 'not less than 75 percent of instruction at public institutions of higher education in the State is provided by tenured or tenure-track faculty.'" See Kevin Carey, "Bernie Sanders's Charming, Perfectly Awful Plan to Save Higher Education," *Chronicle of Higher Education*, July 6, 2015, available at http://chronicle.com/article/Bernie-Sanderss-Charming/231387.

[60] David N. Figlio, Morton O. Schapiro, and Kevin B. Soter, "Are Tenure Track Professors Better Teachers?" NBER Working Paper 19406, National Bureau of Economic Research, Cambridge, MA, September 2013, available at www.nber.org/papers/19406, revised August 28, 2014. See Bowen and Tobin, *Locus of Authority*, pp. 156ff., for further discussion of this subject.

must be the best teachers (which may well be justified when it comes to teaching students how to do research but not otherwise), it is hardly surprising that Figlio and colleagues found that in at least some situations NTT faculty were more effective than their tenured counterparts—and were especially effective with disadvantaged students. After all, there are surely "master teachers" who are less interested in research than in teaching. As Sarah Turner, chair of the economics department at the University of Virginia, said (in personal correspondence): "Such individuals could often do many other things but prefer a satisfying 'life in the classroom.'" The key is to select these teachers well, compensate them appropriately, and treat them with the respect that they deserve.

We are persuaded that higher education should professionalize the "teaching corps" much as many universities professionalized research staff following World War II and the explosive growth of sponsored research that accompanied it. In the immediate postwar years, it became evident that the substantial numbers of highly qualified scientists needed for large-scale research projects could not possibly be accommodated within the regular teaching faculty even though they were indispensable; but it was equally evident that these scientists required status and appropriate conditions of employment. Today there are signs that more and more universities are recognizing the need to regularize conditions of employment for a professional teaching corps. Northwestern, Michigan, and the University of Maryland are among the universities that have taken the lead in this area.[61] Attention to this need is not confined to the research university.

---

[61] Bowen and Tobin, *Locus of Authority*, pp. 157ff., contains references to evolving practice at these institutions as well as a historical discussion of the development of professional research staffs.

Harper College, a forward-looking community college in the Chicago suburbs, has built a system of professional development and regular evaluation for its NTT faculty, and it reports considerable success.[62]

It is not for us to describe in any detail the elements involved in professionalizing the teaching corps (which will, in any case, vary from institution to institution), but we do believe that they should include the following:

* A well-formulated set of titles plus compensation and benefits commensurate with contributions. Northwestern is experimenting with the title "professor of instruction."[63]
* A clear understanding of terms of appointment and opportunities for re-appointment. We do not think that conferring tenure is necessary or appropriate, given needs to preserve staffing flexibility; there are other ways to protect the academic freedom of NTT faculty.
* A well-defined evaluation process that spells out basic protections (rights of appeal) for NTT faculty, who must enjoy the core elements of academic freedom, such as the right to express one's own views on even the most controversial issues.
* Measures to confer dignity and respect on NTT faculty, with, for example, the right to participate in faculty deliberations.

It would also be helpful if the established higher-level entities, such as the American Council on Education (ACE), the

---

[62] McPherson site visit, February 18, 2014.

[63] See Colleen Flaherty, "Professors of Instruction," *Inside Higher Ed*, August 12, 2015, available at www.insidehighered.com/news/2015/08/12/northwestern-us-arts-and-sciences-college-updates-titles-teaching-faculty-and-offers.

Association of American Universities (AAU), the Association of Public and Land Grant Universities (APLU), and the National Association of Independent Colleges and Universities (NAICU), would both welcome and endorse the development of a professionalized teaching corps. The large set of NTT faculty should be regarded as within the mainstream of higher education, not as stepchildren.

A further step, albeit one that is surely some years away, would be the development of graduate programs aimed at the development of professional teachers. (Refer back to the earlier discussion of proposals along this line by Jenkins and others.) It is a bit shocking that so many college faculty are let loose on undergraduates with practically no training in the work of teaching—itself a sign of the regrettably low esteem in which the main work of most universities is held by too many of those who lead and manage them. Preparing instructors to a high standard is demanding and important work for which universities should find a place.

Improving Teaching through Technology: Adaptive Learning

Ongoing advances in information technology offer higher education extremely promising opportunities to improve outcomes *and* control costs. This subject deserves a high place on the agenda for change. In thinking about the potential of technology to help us address the problems we have highlighted in this book, and the potential of online learning in particular, a useful mantra is *distinguish, distinguish, distinguish*—between types of online learning, kinds of courses taught, student populations, and so on. There is so much "noise" in this rapidly evolving area that generalization is hazardous, albeit necessary in limited ways.

One obvious distinction is between MOOCs ("massive open online courses") and other forms of online learning. The age of hyper-adulation of the MOOC has come and gone. To be sure, MOOCs are here to stay—but they are no panacea.[64] They have a useful role to play in reaching learners all over the world and in providing content to individuals of all ages and backgrounds who might otherwise have no access to it. They have proven especially valuable to experienced individuals who have already studied the subjects covered by the MOOCs. But they are not the solution, at least in their present form, to the needs of mainline educational institutions seeking to improve outcomes for their students while reducing or at least controlling costs. They are too blunt an instrument—their very "openness" to learners of all kinds limits drastically their usefulness in specific curricular settings.

ITHAKA made a major effort to test out the capacity of the University System of Maryland to adapt MOOCs created under the Coursera umbrella so that they could meet their most pressing institutional needs at the undergraduate level—increasing completion rates, reducing time-to-degree, and reducing disparities in outcomes while reducing or at least controlling costs. The results were at best mixed; it proved very difficult and very time-consuming, with the best will in the world and full support from both Coursera and the University System of Maryland, to take courses designed to reach a wide array of individual learners

---

[64] See Dan Stober, "MOOCs Haven't Lived Up to the Hopes and the Hype, Stanford Participants Say," *Stanford Report*, October 15, 2015, available at http://news.stanford.edu/news/2015/october/moocs-no-panacea-101515.html. See also the white paper by Alan M. Garber, provost of Harvard, "Everywhere and Anytime, Here and Now: Digital and Residential Education at Harvard," October 2015, http://provost.harvard.edu/files/provost/files/online_learning_whitepaper_final.pdf.

with a one-size-fits-all structure of content and modify them to work in an established curricular context. Lesson learned: it is exceedingly difficult (and expensive) to take a platform designed for one purpose and adapt it to serve quite different purposes.

Consistent with our theme of "distinguish, distinguish, distinguish," we agree with President John Hennessy's prediction regarding other kinds of online teaching:

* Online educational technologies will dominate for certificate and credential-based courses both for skills training and post-graduate professional education.
* Online will play a major role in professional masters programs that do not require/benefit from substantial large-group interaction and student networking.
* Hybrid models will develop: months online + 3–5 days live.[65]

Later in his talk, Hennessy stated his expectation that hybrid models of adaptive learning, as discussed later in this section, will continue to evolve in productive ways. In terms of our focus on BA-granting programs, there is already evidence of at least some success with adaptive learning models.[66]

[65] John Hennessy, "Information Technology and the Future of Teaching and Learning," Robert H. Atwell Lecture, annual meeting of the American Council of Education (ACE), Washington, DC, March 2015. This is a superb presentation that we recommend to all readers. It can be found at http://news.stanford.edu/thedish/2015/03/16/president-john-hennessy-delivers-aces-atwell-lecture/.

[66] A Tyton Partners report by Adam Newman—*Learning to Adapt: A Case for Accelerating Adaptive Learning in Higher Education*, Boston, April 2013—defines adaptive learning as "a more personalized, technology-enabled, and data-driven approach to learning that has the potential to deepen student engagement with learning materials, customize student's' pathways through curriculum, and permit instructors to use class time in more focused and productive ways. In this fashion, adaptive learning promises to make a significant contribution to improving retention, measuring student learning, aiding the achievement of better outcomes, and improving pedagogy." Newman adds, "If adaptive learning solutions are imple-

The most persuasive evidence is from an Ithaka S+R study of a hybrid statistics course (machine-guided instruction à la the Carnegie-Mellon University [CMU] adaptive learning structure plus one face-to-face meeting a week) on six public university campuses that used randomized assignment of students to either a traditional version of the course or the hybrid model in order to control for selection effects. This study found that a carefully designed adaptive learning structure, with multiple feedback loops, can yield essentially the same learning outcomes as a traditional course but with much less face-to-face staff time and less time invested in the course by students. Another key finding was that an important sub-set of students, those who were relatively less prepared academically, did as well with the adaptive learning model as did their better-prepared classmates.[67]

Recent articles on efforts to teach microeconomics via online approaches have reported results that are said to be different from the Ithaka S+R results, but these microeconomics studies used a much simpler type of online learning—one that relied mainly on posting materials on the web and viewing videos and that lacked the key feedback features of more sophisticated, more

mented at scale, then they have the potential—at least theoretically—to produce a higher-quality learning experience (as measured by student engagement, persistence, and outcomes) at potentially reduced cost by making high-quality instruction more scalable" (4–5). The report is available at http://tytonpartners.com/library/accelerating-adaptive-learning-in-higher-education/.

[67] William G. Bowen, Matthew M. Chingos, Kelly A. Lack, and Thomas I. Nygren, "Interactive Learning Online at Public Universities: Evidence from Randomized Trials," Ithaka S+R, New York, 2012, available at http://sr.ithaka.org/sites/default/files/reports/sr-ithaka-interactive-learning-online-at-public-universities.pdf. A version of this report has since been published in the *Journal of Policy Analysis and Management* 33, no. 1 (Winter 2014). Hennessy presents key results of the Ithaka S+R study in the presentation just referenced.

personalized adaptive learning approaches.[68] In short, these "different" results were based on tests of "different" modes of online instruction. The main finding from these other studies is nonetheless important and well worth referencing: these studies found that *purely online courses*, with no face-to-face features (unlike those using the hybrid approach, with one face-to-face meeting per week), resulted in statistically significant reductions in learning outcomes for all students, especially for disadvantaged students. This finding is unsurprising because some contact with teaching staff (with opportunities to ask questions) is obviously important to motivate students—especially disadvantaged students—to "stay with the program."[69]

There is also evidence that the "flipped classroom" approach—whereby students are expected to read basic material, usually available online, before coming to classes that then put more emphasis on discussion and Q&A formats—is particularly beneficial for women and underperforming students. To be sure, this pedagogical approach makes only minimal use of technology, especially as compared with the adaptive learning model that we think holds the most promise. Still, it illustrates that at least some incremental progress can be made by re-examining traditional modes of teaching.[70]

[68] See David J. Deming, Claudia Goldin, Lawrence F. Katz, and Noam Yuchtman, "Can Online Learning Bend the Higher Education Cost Curve?" *American Economic Review: Papers & Proceedings* 105, no. 5 (2015): 496–501, available at http://dx.doi.org/10.1257/aer.p20151024.

[69] Much other research has come to this same conclusion. See, for example, Di Xu and Shanna Smith Jaggars, "Adaptability to Online Learning: Differences across Types of Students and Academic Subject Areas," CCRC Working Paper 54, Community College Research Center, Teachers College, Columbia University, New York, February 2013, available at http://ccrc.tc.columbia.edu/publications/adaptability-to-online-learning.html.

[70] See Carl Straumsheim, "Study Sees Gains for Women, Underperforming Students in Flipped Classroom," *Inside Higher Ed*, September 23, 2015, for a summary of a

Adaptive learning models have much more promise, we believe, even though they need improvement. The modest success of the adaptive learning statistics course that Ithaka S+R tested in a hybrid mode supports the notion that combining a modest amount of face-to-face instruction with the use of extensive feedback loops in the machine-guided mode of teaching works. But this experiment does not imply that the course structure we tested was ideal. It was not. The results are, however, sufficiently promising to persuade us (and, we hope, others) to press on, working to correct the limitations of the statistics course used in our test and to encourage the creation of a prototype adaptive learning platform(s) that could be scaled up and yield highly cost-effective modes of teaching basic content of certain kinds.

This is a good place to emphasize another key distinction: between foundational courses in fields such as statistics in which key concepts are broadly accepted (and where there is "one right answer" to many questions, at least at the beginning level), and courses in fields such as international affairs, in which solutions to problems like the Arab–Israeli conflict defy simplistic "yes or no" answers. The kinds of adaptive learning models we believe have great potential are far better suited to the statistics world than to the Arab–Israeli world. In designing platforms and courses in various fields of study, it is important to avoid "one-size-fits-all" thinking.

Experience with the CMU stats course revealed that its main deficiency was rigidity—it provided no opportunity for user communities to customize the program in any way. For instance, one of the test sites was Baruch College in New York,

study by researchers at Yale University and the University of Massachusetts at Amherst, based on five years' worth of data on an upper-level biochemistry first taught in a traditional model and then "flipped."

and faculty there wanted to include an example that involved the testing of a Christmas pricing experiment at Macy's. This proved impossible to accomplish. More generally, we know that failure to allow some degree of customization is a major barrier to the adoption of adaptive learning platforms; faculty at user sites need some opportunity to contribute to the content of the course they are overseeing.[71]

There is much to be said for innovative attempts to re-engineer complete aspects of the curriculum at many universities (especially those below the resource-rich top-tier publics and privates) to take fuller advantage of what improving information technology can contribute. This is a particularly appealing idea when we compare adaptive learning platforms, recognizing their limitations, with existing modes of delivering content, not with some idealized version of an introductory course taught by inspired faculty and graduate students who enjoy a full command of the English language and have great teaching skills (hardly the norm!). However, we view this "big-picture vision" as overly ambitious and unrealistic, at least at this juncture. It is just too hard to bring about such a sweeping reform now. One problem is that, at present, we lack evidence that an improved adaptive learning platform can really deliver the expected results—in terms of both learning outcomes and cost controls.

The more modest, step-by-step approach that we favor involves concentrating energies and resources on first developing

---

[71] See Lawrence S. Bacow, William G. Bowen, Kevin M. Guthrie, Kelly A. Lack, and Matthew P. Long, "Barriers to Adoption of Online Learning Systems in U.S. Higher Education," Ithaka S+R, New York, May 1, 2012, available at www.sr.ithaka.org/research-publications/barriers-adoption-online-learning-systems-us-higher-education.

and implementing successfully an adaptive learning platform (and associated content) for several basic foundational courses and then, if rigorous evaluation demonstrates that the experiment has been successful, to scale up the effort to include more courses with similar characteristics—and to extend the project to more campuses. If such a proto-typical project were to show good results, it should be possible, as a next step, to encourage other institutions to move in this direction.

There are three reasons for starting out with an effort to improve the teaching of a variant of basic mathematics. First, it is widely acknowledged by leaders in the field that at present basic mathematics is not well taught at many colleges and universities.[72] Second, mathematics lends itself exceptionally well to the adaptive learning approach that we regard as so promising. Third, there is abundant evidence that for many students the need to overcome encounters with basic math requirements is the single most daunting obstacle to earning a college degree within a reasonable period of time.[73] We quoted earlier the wise

---

[72] As noted in the recent report of the President's Council of Advisors on Science and Technology (PCAST), "Engage to Excel," mathematics is seen as the number one barrier to college completion at a time when the nation needs many more mathematics majors, non-majors with more extensive and deeper mathematics preparation, and science, technology, engineering, and mathematics (STEM) majors who are better prepared for the mathematically intensive aspects of the life sciences, social sciences, engineering, information technology, business, and security. See TPSEMath, "Transforming Post-Secondary Education in Mathematics—Report of a Meeting," University of Texas at Austin, June 20–22, 2014, available at https://d3n8a8pro7vhmx.cloudfront.net/math/pages/47/attachments/original/1415904260/TPSE_Report_pages_web.pdf?1415904260.

[73] See Gay M. Clyburn, "Improving on the American Dream: Mathematics Pathways to Student Success," *Change: The Magazine of Higher Learning*, September–October,

words of one experienced observer: "developmental mathematics is where aspirations go to die."

There is certainly no guarantee that an effort of this kind will succeed. We view such an approach as a high-stakes experiment with no assured outcome. Much work needs to be done in configuring this particular effort, and there is no need to go into detail here. The specifics will undoubtedly evolve in ways we cannot predict. Also, there should be many other efforts to serve the same ends. The point to emphasize is that this general approach offers great potential for major progress in addressing the need to improve outcomes at a scale that results in sustainable costs. There is a strong argument, we believe, for making the considerable up-front investment(s) needed to provide a real test of this approach.

Enabling Stronger Leadership

Our discussion of how to take fuller advantage of ever-improving technologies leads directly into the much broader question— the last on our agenda for change—of how to strengthen leader-

---

2013, p. 17, available at www.changemag.org/Archives/Back%20Issues/2013/September-October%202013/american-dream-full.html.

Of course, we all recognize that pre-college education today produces too many students who are not really ready for serious college work. In the longer run, our country simply must do a better job of preparing all of our students, including especially those from disadvantaged backgrounds, to have the opportunity to benefit from at least some kind of post-secondary experience. But we all have only two hands. Important as it is to work on pre-collegiate problems (and some of the ways of improving college teaching, such as the proposed math program, may well help at the pre-college level as well), we cannot wait for some "revolution" at the pre-college level to solve present-day problems. We must all do all that we can to help those now graduating from high school to take full advantage of post-secondary opportunities of various kinds.

ship capacities in higher education. We do not repeat here the list of forces making it harder to exert principled leadership, the examples of the need for change in this area, or the long-ago exhortations of Clark Kerr that we halt the denigration of presidential leadership (all discussed at the end of part II).

We regret to say that we have not identified any simple, over-arching, sure-fire way(s) of correcting this vexing set of problems—especially the pressures against experimentation and risk-taking. Indeed, we are skeptical of proposals for more leadership training or the active promotion of the kinds of leadership development prevalent in the best-run companies, which differ fundamentally from universities in their more hierarchical structure. There is no way of escaping the restraints that disciplinary structure and attendant standards of academic performance impose on the development, selection, and retention of top-flight leadership. Nor should we want to escape the bounds imposed by the very hallmarks of excellence in teaching and scholarship—even as we recognize and applaud the willingness of some colleges and universities to appoint non-traditional candidates to leadership positions. Proposals for more training of trustees and regents deserve careful consideration and might be of at least limited use, but it is important not to encourage excess "activism" on the part of board members.

Trite and even vacuous as it may sound, there is no substitute for two things: (1) a change in mindsets about presidential leadership and (2) a much sharper societal realization that the wrong kinds of external scrutiny and political intrusion can wreak havoc.

Expectations concerning the role of the leaders of educational institutions are important. Given the problems the nation confronts in delivering on the potential of higher education to contribute not only to economic progress but to the advancement of societal values (upward mobility first and foremost), it is not good enough simply to protect "business-as-usual" practices. Presidents should be expected to promote risk-taking and experimentation and should not be afraid to "rock the boat." This is especially true in the area of teaching methods, which must continue to evolve in new ways, with rigorous assessment of what works and what doesn't work at each step along the way. Accompanying changes in staffing patterns (the embrace of a well-qualified teaching corps) are part and parcel of this same set of opportunities. Of course presidents can never be solo performers: they need to build strong teams, and provosts, in particular, need to be strong partners of presidents. Finding and supporting able people in this role is a critical responsibility of the president.[74]

It is much easier to specify needed changes in mindsets than it is to propose concrete ways of selecting excellent candidates and protecting presidents who take risks from being thrown under the bus—except, of course, when they should be! But there are some practices that should be avoided. One is rewarding presidents for playing the "ratings" game (sometimes by providing dollar incentives for achieving increases in the *US News* ratings). Specifically, it is counterproductive to press excessively for increases in standard SAT scores, which are notoriously poor predictors of achievement (in contrast to both achieve-

---

[74] See Lee Gardner, "The Path to Change Runs through the Provost's Office," *Chronicle of Higher Education*, September 8, 2015. Bowen can attest to the power of this proposition on the basis of his experience at Princeton, where he was blessed with a succession of superb provosts, including Sheldon Hackney and Neil Rudenstine, who went on to become the presidents of the University of Pennsylvania and Harvard, respectively.

ment test scores and measures of performance in secondary school) and which can discourage the enrollment of poor-testing but high-potential students, including many from disadvantaged backgrounds. It is also counterproductive to emphasize the desirability of maintaining certain input measures, such as teacher–student ratios, when embracing measures that entail trade-offs that push against high teacher–student ratios can be necessary to increase cost-effectiveness. We know of a particular case in which an able president decided against changes that he believed would enhance cost-effectiveness precisely because he feared the reaction of both his board and potential students to a possible reduction in ratings.[75]

The president and board of a broad-access institution need to be careful about setting up performance metrics that may run counter to the institution's mission. The two easiest ways to increase graduation rates are to turn away less qualified students and to lower graduation standards. The right challenge for the institution is to increase the graduation rate for students with proper qualifications while maintaining the rigor of graduation standards.

---

[75] More generally, we are skeptical about the wisdom of trying to create rating or ranking systems for higher education. It is so easy to send the wrong signals and to create the wrong incentives. The US Department of Higher Education has wisely backed off efforts to create a one-dimensional ranking system. Also, efforts to use Pell Grant numbers to measure the commitment of institutions to reducing disparities in outcomes miss the effects of differences among institutions in geographic location. California institutions do so well on such rankings in part because they have at hand pools of Asian Americans who are well qualified but who come from low-income families. The demographic situation of places like the University of Virginia could not be more different. Most of the things raters want to measure are a product both of an institution's efforts and its circumstances; once ratings are promulgated, the temptation is to assume that the institution is entirely responsible for the results. (There have been years in Chicago when a sitting mayor was in effect blamed for a particularly bad series of snowstorms. This did not end well.)

There is no substitute for understanding well the business you are in—and an important responsibility for a president is to find ways to educate the board about the really meaningful indicators of progress for the institution.

It is of course important to select as president as able a person as can be found. A well-qualified board needs to take an active role in the search process and not be too dependent on either search firms that may have their own agendas or current faculty (who may need to be upgraded by stronger leadership than they would welcome). We are also unmoved, indeed negatively inclined, toward proposals to attract a new person by paying an outsized salary. A president should of course be compensated adequately. But a salary that many sensible people will regard as grossly excessive can be a thorn in the side of a president—as can outlandish expenditures on presidential housing and, in one widely publicized case, a dog run. A president is well served by eschewing "perks" that interfere with the notion that "we are all in this together."

A board should also resist over-wrought worries about "administrative bloat" (debunked in an earlier section of this book) and encourage the president to appoint the key support staff the institution needs to succeed. We favor a lean management structure with relatively few levels of delegation, but preferences in this regard obviously vary, as they should, according to both personalities and circumstances. The key is to give the president some leeway in devising a structure that will work well in his or her circumstances. More generally, creating an environment in which strong leadership is supported is very important.

Strong presidential leadership can also be encouraged by periodic (annual) reviews of the president's performance, which often lead to valuable suggestions for improvements in one or another aspect of presidential leadership. Regular executive sessions, sans the president, at the end of each board meeting can serve the same purpose. There is, finally, no substitute for an effective partnership between the president or chancellor and the board chair. The absence of such a "partnership" can be devastating (as the saga of Cooper Union reveals).

Even more ominous is the evidence that intrusion by politically active attorneys general can be damaging. Both the Cooper Union and the Sweet Briar College situations are vivid reminders that even private colleges can be held hostage to sloganeering ("free tuition" at Cooper Union) and reluctance to seem in any way insensitive to the needs of women (Sweet Briar). A blindness to economic realities is not a good path forward. The struggle of Chancellor Rebecca M. Blank in Wisconsin against Governor Scott Walker's efforts to remake the University of Wisconsin is an equally vivid reminder of the even greater risks to public universities of the wrong kinds of "attention." As a society, we have yet to find the right balance between the need to monitor the performance of boards, as well as presidents, and the need to avoid protracted, overly personal, overtly publicized conflicts that serve no compelling educational purpose.

Naïve as it may be to say this, we have to regain the notion that presidential leadership is a noble calling—it is! One thing that would help in this regard is better journalistic coverage of higher education. We seem to be in a period when even highly respected papers like the *New York Times* are inclined to publish truly foolish pieces that exaggerate problems—if they do not simply invent them. (As President Brian Rosenberg of Macalester College wryly observed, maybe the *Times* would be interested in a piece by him titled "College Causes Cancer."[76]) Of course we are aware that problems of this kind are driven by both the changing economics of publishing and the political polarization of the world in which we live.

Ideally, and we can still harbor this hope, higher education at its best will produce graduates who will resist foolishness of all kinds—and colleges and universities will continue to be homes for responsible faculty critics of every point of view. Such lofty aspirations can be combined, absolutely properly, with a renewed determination to serve seemingly mundane goals such as improved levels of educational attainment at affordable cost, as well as a re-engagement with pressing national issues of inequality and social mobility. As Thoreau observed: "In the long run, men hit only what they aim at. Therefore, they had better aim at something high."

[76] See Brian Rosenberg, "What Has Happened to 'The New York Times?'" *Inside Higher Ed*, June 11, 2015, available at www.insidehighered.com/views/2015/06/11/essay-criticizes-pieces-new-york-times-publishing-higher-education.

References

Abel, Jaison R., and Richard Deitz. "Do the Benefits of College Still Out-weigh the Costs?" *Current Issues in Economy and Finance* 20, no. 3 (Federal Reserve Bank of New York, 2014). Available at www.new yorkfed.org/research/current_issues/ci20-3.pdf.

Alon, Sigal. *Race, Class and Affirmative Action*. New York: Russell Sage Foundation, 2015.

Arum, Richard, and Josipa Roksa. *Academically Adrift: Limited Learning on College Campuses*. Chicago: University of Chicago Press, 2011.

Astin, Alexander. "The Promise and Peril of Outcomes Assessment." *Chronicle of Higher Education*, September 3, 2013.

Autor, David. "Skills, Education, and the Rise of Earnings Inequality among the 'Other 99 Percent.'" *Science*, May 2014.

———. "Polanyi's Paradox and the Shape of Employment Growth." Draft prepared for the Federal Bank of Kansas City's economic policy sym-posium Re-evaluating Labor Market Dynamics, August 21–23, 2014, in Jackson Hole, Wyoming. Available at http://economics.mit.edu/files/9835.

Avery, Christopher, and Sarah Turner. "Are Students Borrowing Too Much—or Not Enough?" *Journal of Economic Perspectives* 26, no. 1 (2012): 165–92.

Bacow, Lawrence S., and William G. Bowen. "The Real Work of 'Saving' 2 Colleges Has Yet to Be Done." *Chronicle of Higher Education*, Septem-ber 8, 2015. Available at http://chronicle.com/article/The-Real-Work -of-Saving-/232901/?cid=at&utm_source=at&utm_medium=en.

———. "Double Trouble: Sweet Briar College and Cooper Union." Ithaka S+R issue brief, September 21, 2015. Available at www.sr.ithaka.org/blog/double-trouble/.

———. "The Painful Lessons of Sweet Briar and Cooper Union." *Chronicle of Higher Education*, September 24, 2015. Available at http://chronicle .com/article/The-Painful-Lessons-of-Sweet/233369/.

Bacow, Lawrence S., William G. Bowen, Kevin M. Guthrie, Kelly A. Lack, and Matthew P. Long. "Barriers to Adoption of Online Learning Systems in U.S. Higher Education." Ithaka S+R, New York, May 1, 2012. Available at www.sr.ithaka.org/research-publications/barriers-adoption -online-learning-systems-us-higher-education.

Bailey, Martha J., and Susan M. Dynarski. "Gains and Gaps: Changing Inequality in U.S. College Entry and Completion." NBER Working Paper 17633. National Bureau of Economic Research, Cambridge, MA, December 2011.

Bailey, Thomas, Dong Wok Jeong, and Sun-Woo Cho. "Student Progression through Developmental Sequences in Community Colleges." *CCRC Brief* 45 (September 2010).

Basken, Paul. "U.S. May Need to Prune Number of Research Universities, Lobby Group Says." *Chronicle of Higher Education*, June 26, 2009. Available at http://chronicle.com/article/US-May-Need-to-Prune -Number/47339.

Baum, Sandy. "Grad-School Loan Binge Fans Debt Worries." *Wall Street Journal*, August 18, 2015.

Baum, Sandy, and Jennifer Ma. *Trends in College Pricing 2015*. New York: College Board.

Baum, Sandy, and Kathleen Payea. *Education Pays: The Benefits of Higher Education for Individuals and Society*. New York: College Board, 2004. Available at www.collegeboard.com/prod_downloads/press/cost04/ EducationPays2004.pdf.

Baum, Sandy, Alisa Federico Cunningham, and Courtney Tanenbaum. "Educational Attainment: Understanding the Data." Working paper, Graduate School of Education and Human Development, George Washington University, Washington, DC, April 2015. Available at http://gsehd.gwu.edu/sites/default/files/documents/Educational _Attainment_FINAL_Report_4.27.pdf.

Baum, Sandy, Jennifer Ma, and Kathleen Payea. *Education Pays 2013: The Benefits of Higher Education for Individuals and Society*. New York: College Board, 2013.

Bennet, Nathan. "Our Leader Left, Who's Left to Lead?" *Chronicle of Higher Education*, July 22, 2015.

Berelson, Bernard. *Graduate Education in the United States*. New York: McGraw Hill, 1960.

Bernard, Tara Siegel. "The Many Pitfalls of Private Student Loans." *New York Times*, September 4, 2015. Available at www.nytimes.com/2015/

09/05/your-money/student-loans/the-many-pitfalls-of-private-stu dent-loans.html?_r=0.

Berry, Dan. "Notre Dame Stands Firm Amid Shifts in College Athletics." *New York Times*, September 10, 2015.

Bharucha, Jamshed. *The State of Cooper Union*. New York: Cooper Union, March 2013. Available at www.support.cooper.edu/s/1289/images/ editor_documents/support_cooper/thestateofcu0315.pdf.

Bienen, Henry S. "Private Colleges Wouldn't Pay for Play." *BloombergView. com*, September 9, 2015.

Blumenstyk, Goldie. "President Obama to Announce a New 'College Promise' Campaign." *Chronicle of Higher Education*, September 9, 2015. Available at http://chronicle.com/blogs/ticker/president-obama -to-announce-a-new-college-promise-campaign/104269.

Bound, John, Michael F. Lovenheim, and Sarah Turner. "Increasing Time to Baccalaureate Degree in the United States." Population Studies Center Research Report 10–698, University of Michigan, Ann Arbor, April 2010.

Bowen, William G. "Technology: Its Potential Impact on the National Need to Improve Educational Outcomes and Control Costs." Paper pre sented at the DeLange Conference, Rice University, October 13, 2014. Available at www.sr.ithaka.org/publications/technology-its-potential -impact-on-the-national-need-to-improve-educational-outcomes -and-control-costs/.

———. "Academia Online: Musings (Some Unconventional)." Stafford Lit tle Lecture, Princeton University, Princeton, NJ, October 14, 2013.

———. *Higher Education in the Digital Age*. Princeton, NJ: Princeton Uni versity Press, 2013.

———. "Technology: Its Potential Impact on the National Need to Im prove Educational Outcomes and Control Costs." Paper presented at the DeLange Conference, Rice University, October 13, 2014. Avail able at www.sr.ithaka.org/publications/technology-its-potential-impact -on-the-national-need-to-improve-educational-outcomes-and -control-costs/.

Bowen, William G., and Derek Bok. *The Shape of the River: Long-Term Consequences of Considering Race in College and University Admis sions*. Princeton, NJ: Princeton University Press, 1998.

Bowen, William G., and Sarah Levin. *Reclaiming the Game: College Sports and Educational Values*. Princeton, NJ: Princeton University Press, 2005.

Bowen, William G., and Neil L. Rudenstine. *In Pursuit of the PhD*. Prince ton, NJ: Princeton University Press, 1992.

Bowen, William G., and James Shulman. *The Game of Life: College Sports and Educational Values* (Princeton, NJ: Princeton University Press, 2002).

Bowen, William G., and Eugene M. Tobin. *Locus of Authority: The Evolution of Faculty Roles in the Governance of Higher Education*. Princeton, NJ: Princeton University Press, 2015.

Bowen, William G., Matthew M. Chingos, and Michael S. McPherson. *Crossing the Finish Line: Completing College at America's Public Universities*. Princeton, NJ: Princeton University Press, 2009.

Bowen, William G., Martin A. Kurzweil, and Eugene M. Tobin. *Equity and Excellence in American Higher Education*. Charlottesville, VA: University of Virginia Press, 2005.

Bowen, William G., Matthew M. Chingos, Kelly A. Lack, and Thomas I. Nygren. "Interactive Learning Online at Public Universities: Evidence from Randomized Trials." Ithaka S+R, New York, 2012. Available at http://sr.ithaka.org/sites/default/files/reports/sr-ithaka-interactive-learning-online-at-public-universities.pdf. A version of this report has since been published in the *Journal of Policy Analysis and Management* 33, no. 1 (Winter 2014).

Bradley, Ken. "Months after Being Killed, UAB Football Reinstated." *Sporting News*, June 1, 2015, available at www.sportingnews.com/ncaa-football/story/2015-06-01/uab-football-reinstated-rumors-ray-watts-program-returns-killed-birmingham.

Brewer, Dominic, and Patrick McEwan, eds. *Economics of Education*. San Diego, CA: Elsevier Press, 2010.

Brewer, Dominic J., Susan M. Gates, and Charles J. Goldman. *In Pursuit of Prestige: Strategy and Competition in U.S. Higher Education*. New Brunswick, NJ: Transaction Publishers, 2004.

Carey, Kevin. "Bernie Sanders's Charming, Perfectly Awful Plan to Save Higher Education." *Chronicle of Higher Education*, July 6, 2015. Available at http://chronicle.com/article/Bernie-Sanderss-Charming/231387.

———. "Student Debt Is Worse than You Think." *New York Times*, October 7, 2015.

Carnegie Commission on Higher Education. *Ph.D's and the Academic Labor Market*. New York: McGraw Hill, 1976.

Cartter, Allan M. "The Academic Labor Market." In *Higher Education and the Labor Market*. New York: McGraw Hill, 1974. Pp. 281–307.

Cassuto, Leonard. "Why We Need to Remember the Doctorate-of-Arts Degree." *Chronicle of Higher Education*, September 9, 2015.

———. *The Graduate School Mess: What Caused It and How We Can Fix It*. Cambridge, MA: Harvard University Press, 2015.

Chetty, Raj, Nathaniel Hendren, Patrick Kline, Emmanuel Saez, and Nicholas Turner. "Is the United States Still a Land of Opportunity? Recent Trends in Intergenerational Mobility." *American Economic Review* 104, no. 5 (May 2014): 141–47.

Chingos, Matthew M., and Susan M. Dynarski. "How Can We Track Trends in Educational Attainment by Parental Income? Hint: Not with the Current Population Survey." *Brown Center Chalkboard*, Brookings Institution, Washington, DC, March 12, 2015.

Clyburn, Gay M. "Improving on the American Dream: Mathematics Pathways to Student Success." *Change: The Magazine of Higher Learning*, September–October 2013. Available at www.changemag.org/Archives/Back%20Issues/2013/September-October%202013/american-dream-full.html.

College Board. *Trends in College Pricing 2015*.

———. *Trends in Student Aid 2014*. New York.

———. *Annual Survey of Colleges*. New York, 2015.

———. *Trends in Student Aid 2015*. New York.

Committee on Research Universities, Board on Higher Education and Workforce, Policy and Global Affairs. *Research Universities and the Future of America: Ten Breakthrough Actions Vital to Our Nation's Prosperity and Security*. Washington, DC: National Academies Press, 2012. Available at http://sites.nationalacademies.org/pga/bhew/researchuniversities/.

de Tocqueville, Alexis. *Democracy in America*, vol. 1, chapter VIII.

Dee, Thomas. "Are There Civic Returns to Education?" *Journal of Public Economics* 2004, no. 88 (9–10): 1697–1720.

Delbanco, Andrew. "Our Universities: The Outrageous Reality." *New York Review of Books*, July 9, 2015.

DeLisle, Jason, and Alexander Holt. "Zero Marginal Cost: Measuring Subsidies for Graduate Education in the Public Service Loan Forgiveness Program." New America Foundation, Washington, DC, September 2014. Available at www.edcentral.org/wp-content/uploads/2014/09/ZeroMarginalCost_140910_DelisleHolt.pdf.

Deming, David J., Claudia Goldin, and Lawrence F. Katz. "The For-Profit Postsecondary School Sector: Nimble Critters or Agile Predators?" *Journal of Economic Perspectives* 26, no. 1 (Winter 2012): 139–64.

Deming, David J., Claudia Goldin, Lawrence F. Katz, and Noam Yuchtman. "Can Online Learning Bend the Higher Education Cost Curve?" *American Economic Review: Papers & Proceedings* 105, no. 5 (2015): 496–501. Available at http://dx.doi.org/10.1257/aer.p20151024.

Doti, James L. "In Praise of Federal Loans for College." *Chronicle of Higher Education*, July 21, 2015. Available at http://chronicle.com/article/In-Praise-of-Federal-Loans-for/231505?cid=megamenu.

Drape, Joe. "Alabama Is Rolling in Cash, with Tide Lifting All Boats." *New York Times*, November 5, 2015. Available at www.nytimes.com/2015/11/07/sports/ncaafootball/alabama-crimson-tide-football-marketing.html?_r=0.

Duckworth, Angela L., Christopher Peterson, Michael D. Matthews, and Dennis R. Kelly. "Grit: Perseverance and Passion for Long-Term Goals." *Journal of Personality and Social Psychology* 92, no. 6 (2007): 1087–1101.

Dynarski, Susan. "For the Poor, the Graduation Gap Is Even Wider than the Enrollment Gap." *The Upshot, New York Times*, June 2, 2015.

———. "Why Students with the Smallest Debts Have the Larger Problem." *New York Times*, August 31, 2015.

———. "New Data Gives Clearer Picture of Student Debt." *The Upshot, New York Times*, September 10, 2015.

Etchemendy, John. "Are Our Colleges and Universities Failing Us?" *Carnegie Reporter* 7, no. 3 (Winter 2014).

Fain, Paul. "College Completion Rates Decline More Rapidly." *Inside Higher Ed*, November 17, 2015. Available at www.insidehighered.com/quick takes/2015/11/17/college-completion-rates-decline-more-rapidly.

Figlio, David N., Morton O. Schapiro, and Kevin B. Soter. "Are Tenure Track Professors Better Teachers?" NBER Working Paper 19406, National Bureau of Economic Research, Cambridge, MA, September 2013. Available at www.nber.org/papers/19406. Revised August 28, 2014.

Field, Kelly. "6 Years in and 6 to Go, Only Modest Progress on Obama's College-Completion Goal." *Chronicle of Higher Education*, January 20, 2015.

Gaul, Gilbert M. *Billion Dollar Ball: A Journey through the Big-Money Culture of College Football*. New York: Random House, 2015.

Flaherty, Colleen. "5-Year Plan." *Inside Higher Ed*, May 28, 2014. Available at www.insidehighered.com/news/2014/05/28/mla-report-calls-phd -program-reform-including-cutting-time-degree.

———. "Professors of Instruction." *Inside Higher Ed*, August 12, 2015. Available at www.insidehighered.com/news/2015/08/12/northwestern -us-arts-and-sciences-college-updates-titles-teaching-faculty-and -offers.

———. "Hope in Wisconsin." *Inside Higher Ed*, September 8, 2015. Available at www.insidehighered.com/news/2015/09/08/faculty-members -think-massive-donation-will-help-retain-top-professors-u-wisconsin.

Fleischer, Victor. "Stop Universities From Hoarding Money." *New York Times*, August 19, 2015.

Garber, Alan M. "Everywhere and Anytime, Here and Now: Digital and Residential Education at Harvard." October 2015. Available at http://pro vost.harvard.edu/files/provost/files/online_learning_whitepaper_ final.pdf.

Gardner, John W. "Uncritical Lovers, Unloving Critics." Commencement address given at Cornell University, Ithaca, NY, June 1, 1968. Published in *Journal of Education Research* 62, no. 9 (May–June 1969).

Gardner, Lee. "The Path to Change Runs through the Provost's Office." *Chronicle of Higher Education*, September 8, 2015.

Goldin, Claudia, and Lawrence F. Katz. *The Race between Education and Technology*. Cambridge, MA: Harvard University Press, 2008.

Gutmann, Amy, and Dennis Thompson. *The Spirit of Compromise: Why Governing Demands It and Campaigning Undermines It*. Princeton, NJ: Princeton University Press, 2012.

Hennessy, John. "Information Technology and the Future of Teaching and Learning." Robert H. Atwell Lecture, annual meeting of the American Council of Education (ACE), Washington, DC, March 2015, 2015. Available at http://news.stanford.edu/thedish/2015/03/16/president -john-hennessy-delivers-aces-atwell-lecture/.

Herschbein, Brad, and Melissa S. Kearney., "Major Decisions: What Graduates Earn over Their Lifetimes." Economic Analysis. The Hamilton Project, Washington, DC, September 29, 2014.

Hess, Frederick M., Mark Schneider, Andrew P. Kelly, and Kevin Carey. "Diplomas and Dropouts." *American Enterprise Institute*, June 3, 2009. Available at www.aei.org/publication/diplomas-and-dropouts/.

Hoxby, Caroline M., and Sarah E. Turner. "Expanding College Opportunity for High-Achieving, Low-Income Students." Stanford Institute for Economic Policy Research, 2013. Available at http://siepr.stanford.edu.

Hunt, Albert H. "Arne Duncan, Education Secretary, Sees Challenges for U.S. Colleges." *New York Times*, November 8, 2015.

Hussar, William J., and Tabitha M. Bailey. *Projections of Education Statistics to 2022* (Washington, DC: NCES, 2014). Available at http://nces .ed.gov/pubs2014/2014051.pdf.

Institute of Education Sciences (IES). "Postsecondary Attainment: Differences by Socioeconomic Status." *The Condition of Education— Spotlights*, 2015.

———. *Digest of Education Statistics, 2012*. Washington, DC. Available at https://nces.ed.gov/programs/digest/2012menu_tables.asp.

———. *Digest of Education Statistics, 2013*. Washington, DC. Available at https://nces.ed.gov/programs/digest/2013menu_tables.asp.

———. *Digest of Education Statistics, 2014*. Washington, DC. Available at https://nces.ed.gov/programs/digest/2014menu_tables.asp.

Jarvie, Jenny. "University in Alabama Ends Football Program, Angering Just About Everyone." *Los Angeles Times*, December 31, 2014. Available at www.latimes.com/nation/la-na-alabama-football-20141231-story.html.

Jenkins, Rob. "Stop Resisting a 2-Tier System." *Chronicle of Higher Education*, September 28, 2015.

Kane, Thomas J., Peter Orszag, and David L. Gunter. "Funding Restrictions at Public Universities: Effects and Policy Implications." Working paper, Brookings Institution, Washington, DC, 2003. Available at www.brookings.edu/views/papers/orszag/20030910.pdf.

———. "State Fiscal Constraints and Higher Education Spending: The Role of Medicaid and the Business Cycle." The Urban Institute, May 2003.

———. "Politics, and the Ouster of a Popular President: Cloud UNC's Search for a New Leader." *Chronicle of Higher Education*, June 11, 2015. Available at http://chronicle.com/article/Politicsthe-Ouster-of-a/230825/.

Kelderman, Eric. "NLRB's Northwestern Ruling Sets a High Bar for Approving Student-Athlete Unions," *Chronicle of Higher Education*, August 18, 2015. Available at http://chronicle.com/article/NLRB-s -Northwestern-Ruling/232441/.

———. "Where Scott Walker Got His Utilitarian View of Higher Education— and Why It Matters." *Chronicle of Higher Education*, September 2, 2015. Available at http://chronicle.com/article/Where-Scott-Walker -Got-His/232803/.

Kerr, Clark. *The Uses of the University*, 4th ed. The Godkin Lectures on the Essentials of Free Government and the Duties of the Citizen. Cambridge, MA: Harvard University Press, 1995.

Leonhardt, David. "The Reality of Student Debt Is Different From the Clichés." *The Upshot, New York Times*, July 24, 2014. Available at www .nytimes.com/2014/06/24/upshot/the-reality-of-student-debt-is-dif ferent-from-the-cliches.html?_r=0&abt=0002&abg=0.

Long, Bridget Terry. "The Financial Crisis and College Enrollment: How Have Students and Their Families Responded?" In *How the Financial Crisis and Great Recession Affected Higher Education*, edited by Jeffrey R. Brown and Caroline M. Hoxby. Chicago: University of Chicago Press, 2015.

Long, Bridget T., and Michal Kurlaender. "Do Community Colleges Provide a Viable Pathway to a Baccalaureate Degree?" *Educational Evaluation and Policy Analysis* 15, no. 1 (2015): 30–53.

Lumina Foundation. *A Stronger Nation through Higher Education*, 2014 edition. Indianapolis.

McPherson, Michael S., and Morton O. Schapiro. *The Student Aid Game*. Princeton, NJ: Princeton University Press, 1998.

———. *The Student Aid Game: Meeting Need and Rewarding Talent in American Higher Education*. Princeton, NJ: Princeton University Press, 1999.

———. "Funding Roller Coaster for Public Higher Education," *Science* 302, no. 5648 (2003): 1157.

Michel, Lawrence. "Causes of Wage Stagnation." Economic Policy Institute, Washington DC, January 6, 2015. Available at www.epi.org/publication/causes-of-wage-stagnation/.

Moretti, Enrico. "Estimating the Social Return to Higher Education: Evidence from Longitudinal and Repeated Cross-Sectional Data." *Journal of Econometrics* 121 (2004): 175–212.

Mulhern, Christine, Richard R. Spies, Matthew P. Staiger, and D. Derek Wu. "The Effects of Rising Student Costs in Higher Education: Evidence from Public Institutions in Virginia." Ithaka S+R research publication, March 4, 2015. Available at http://sr.ithaka.org/research-publications/effects-rising-student-costs-higher-education.

National Center for Education Statistics (NCES). "Education Longitudinal Study of 2002" (ELS:2002). Base Year and Third Follow-up. Washington, DC.

———. *The Condition of Education 2012.* NCES 2012–045. Washington, DC.

———. *National Postsecondary Student Aid Study*, 2012. Washington, DC.

———. *Digest of Educational Statistics, 2014.* Washington, DC. Available at https://nces.ed.gov/programs/digest/d14/tables/dt14_307.10.asp?current=yes.

———. "Trends in Undergraduate Nonfederal Grant and Scholarship Aid by Demographic and Enrollment Characteristics, Selected Years 1999–2000 to 2011–2012." NCES 2015–604. Washington, DC, September 2015. Available at http://nces.ed.gov/pubs2015/2015604.pdf.

National Student Clearinghouse (NSC). *Completing College: A National View of Student Attainment Rates—Fall 2008 Cohort.* Signature Report. Herndon, VA: November 2014.

Newman, Adam. *Learning to Adapt: A Case for Accelerating Adaptive Learning in Higher Education.* Tyton Partners report, Boston, April 2013. Available at http://tytonpartners.com/library/accelerating-adaptive-learning-in-higher-education/.

Organisation for Economic Co-operation and Development (OECD). *Education at a Glance Interim Report: Update of Employment and Educational Attainment Indicators.* Paris, January 2015. Available at www.oecd.org/edu/eag.htm.

Oxtoby, David. "Endowments Are Financial Pillars, Not Piggy Banks." *Chronicle of Higher Education*, September 21, 2015.

Patel, Vimal. "How the U. of Missouri Became a Hotbed for Graduate Student Activism." *Chronicle of Higher Education*, September 4, 2015.

Perna, Laura W. "Understanding the Working Student." *Academe*, July–August 2010.

Putnam, Robert D. *Our Kids: The American Dream in Crisis.* New York: Simon and Schuster, 2015.

Roderick, Melissa, Jenny Nagaoka, Vanessa Coca, and Eliza Moeller. "From High to the Future: Making Hard Work Pay Off." Consortium on Chicago School Research, April 2009.

Roderick, Melissa, Jenny Nagaoka, Vanessa Coca, Eliza Moeller, Karen Roddie, Jamiliyah Gilliam, and Desmond Patton. "From High School to the Future: Potholes on the Road to College." Consortium on Chicago School Research, March 2008.

Rosenbaum, James E., and Janet Rosenbaum. "Beyond BA Blinders: Lessons from Occupational Colleges and Certificate Programs for Nontraditional Students." *Journal of Economic Perspectives* 27, no. 2 (Spring 2013): 153–72.

Rosenberg, Brian. "What Has Happened to 'The New York Times?'" *Inside Higher Ed*, June 11, 2015. Aavailable at www.insidehighered.com/views/2015/06/11/essay-criticizes-pieces-new-york-times-publishing-higher-education.

———. "My William Deresiewicz Problem." *Chronicle of Higher Education*, September 2, 2015.

Ross-Sorkin, Andrew, and Megan Thee-Brennan. "Many Feel American Dream Is Out of Reach, Poll Shows." *New York Times*, December 11, 2014. Available at http://dealbook.nytimes.com/2014/12/10/many-feel-the-american-dream-is-out-of-reach-poll-shows/?_r=0.

Sandeen, Cathy. "Here's What I Learned from the Near-Death of a Small College." *Time*, July 3, 2015.

Siegel, Lee. "Why I Defaulted on My Student Loans." *New York Times*, June 6, 2015. Available at www.nytimes.com/2015/06/07/opinion/sunday/why-i-defaulted-on-my-student-loans.html?_r=0.

Stiglitz, Joseph E. *Rewriting the Rules of the American Economy: An Agenda for Growth and Shared Prosperity*. New York: W. W. Norton, November 2015.

Stratford, Michael. "Lumina-Funded Paper Proposes Federal 'Risk-Sharing' Accountability System." *Inside Higher Education*, September 9, 2015.

Stober, Dan. "MOOCs Haven't Lived Up to the Hopes and the Hype, Stanford Participants Say." *Stanford Report*, October 15, 2015. Available at http://news.stanford.edu/news/2015/october/moocs-no-panacea-101515.html.

Straumsheim, Carl. "Study Sees Gains for Women, Underperforming Students in Flipped Classroom." *Inside Higher Education*, September 23, 2015.

Stripling, Jack. "Stage Is Set for Uncommon Ugliness in Illinois Chancellor's Exit." *Chronicle of Higher Education*, August 13, 2015. Available at http://chronicle.com/article/Stage-Is-Set-for-Uncommon/232379/.

Supiano, Beckie. "Financial Literacy: Can It Be Taught? Should Colleges Even Try?" *Chronicle of Higher Education*, July 17, 2015. Available at http://chronicle.com/article/Financial-Literacy-Can-It-Be/231691/.

Thomason, Andy. "Even Private Colleges Feel the Pain as Enrollment Falls Again." *Chronicle of Higher Education*, May 14, 2015.

———. "'Angry Olives' Game Skewers U. of Akron's President." *Inside Higher Education*, September 25, 2015.

———. "Small Colleges' Closure Rate Could Triple by 2017, Moody's Says." *Chronicle of Higher Education*, September 25, 2015.

TPSEMath. *Transforming Post-Secondary Education in Mathematics—Report of a Meeting*, University of Texas at Austin, June 20–22, 2014. Available at https://d3n8a8pro7vhmx.cloudfront.net/math/pages/47/attachments/original/1415904260/TPSE_Report_pages_web.pdf?1415904260.

Trow, Martin. "Problems in the Transition from Elite to Mass Higher Education," Carnegie Commission on Higher Education, Berkeley, CA, 1973.

Turner, Sarah E. "Going to College and Finishing College." In *College Choices: The Economics of Where to Go, and How to Pay For It*, edited by Caroline M. Hoxby. Cambridge, MA: National Bureau of Economic Research, September 2004).

———. "The Impact of the Financial Crisis on Faculty Labor Markets." In *How the Financial Crisis and Great Recession Affected Higher Education*, edited by Jeffrey R. Brown and Caroline M. Hoxby. Chicago: University of Chicago Press, 2015.

US Bureau of Labor Statistics. *National Longitudinal Survey of Youth*, 1979 and 1997. Washington, DC. Available at www.nlsinfo.org/content/cohorts/nlsy79 and https://www.nlsinfo.org/content/cohorts/nlsy97.

US Census Bureau and Bureau of Labor Statistics. *Current Population Survey*. Washington, DC: 2015. Available at www.census.gov/cps/.

Vanness, David J. "The Withering of a Once-Great State University." *Chronicle of Higher Education*, July 13, 2015. Available at http://chronicle.com/article/The-Withering-of-a-Once-Great/231565/.

Weissman, Jordan. "The *New York Times* Should Apologize for the Awful Op-Ed It Just Ran on Student Loans." *Slate*, June 8, 2015. Available at www.slate.com/blogs/moneybox/2015/06/08/lee_siegel_new_york_times_op_ed_is_this_the_worst_op_ed_ever_written_about.html.

White, Dan. *Crowded Out: The Outlook for State Higher Education Spending*. Moody's Analytics, April 21, 2015.

Woodhouse, Kellie. "A Career's Worth of Change." *Inside Higher Ed*, July 14, 2015. Available at www.insidehighered.com/news/2015/07/14/

exit-interview-outgoing-university-system-maryland-chancellor
-brit-kirwan.

Xu, Di, and Shanna Smith Jaggars. "Adaptability to Online Learning: Differences across Types of Students and Academic Subject Areas." CCRC Working Paper 54, Community College Research Center, Teachers College, Columbia University, New York, February 2013. Available at http://ccrc.tc.columbia.edu/publications/adaptability-to-online
-learning.html.

Zakaria, Fareed. "Why America's Obsession with STEM Education Is Dangerous." *Washington Post*, March 26, 2015.

Zimmerman, Seth D. "The Returns to College Admission for Academically Marginal Students." *Journal of Labor Economics*, October 2014, pp. 711–54.

Index

Page numbers for entries occurring in figures are followed by an *f*; those for entries in notes, by an *n*; and those for entries in tables, by a *t*.

students: admissions criteria for, 95–96, 136–37; choosing colleges and majors, 9n9, 101–2; coping skills of, 96; dependent, 52–57; dropouts, 23–24; employment during college, 6n6, 24, 33–34, 60, 97; genders, 17–18; independent, 24, 52, 54, 55; investment in education by, 3–4; matches with institutions, 26–29; part-time, 6n6; perseverance of, 22; SAT scores of, 95–96, 136–37; services for, 47. *See also* race and ethnicity; socioeconomic status

Supiano, Becky, 60n77

Sweet Briar College, ix, 18n12, 65, 67, 139

Tanenbaum, Courtney, 15–16, 15n7

taxes: on college graduates, 7, 7–8n7; on higher income groups, 74; state, 78, 80–81, 82–83

teaching: future evolution of, 136; research on, 86, 123–24; skills of, 113–14, 115, 116n48, 123–24, 126; unbundling responsibilities of, 122n58. *See also* online learning

teaching corps, 124–26, 136. *See also* faculty members

technology: automation, 20, 108–9; educational investments and, 4; instructional, 70–71. *See also* online learning

tertiary education. *See* graduate programs; higher education

Thee-Brennan, Megan, 36n45

Thomason, Andy, 18n12, 66n85, 68n87

Thompson, Dennis, 62n81

Thoreau, Henry David, 140

Thorp, Holden, 120

time-to-degree: consequences of, 32, 34, 97; disparities by socioeconomic status, 33–34, 42n51; factors in, 30, 31–34, 60, 89–90; in PhD programs, 112, 115; reducing, 116–18; trends in, 31; tuition costs and, 32, 89–90. *See also* college completion rates

Tinto, Vincent, 117n50

Tobin, Eugene M., 34–35n44, 70nn90–91, 122n57, 123n60, 124n61

Tobin, James, 99–100n31

Tocqueville, Alexis de, 3, 3n2

TPSEMath (Transforming Post-Secondary Education in Mathematics), 86

Trow, Martin, 92, 92n19

trustees: decisions to close colleges, 65–66, 67, 88; outside pressures on, 66–67; relations with presidents, 137–39; selecting presidents, 138; support of college sports, 120; training of, 135. *See also* leadership

tuition costs: at community colleges, 26, 50, 90n18, 91; for dependent students, 52–57, 53t; free, 26, 87–91, 90n18; by income quartile, 43–44, 52–57, 53t; for independent students, 54, 55; by institution type, 48–50, 49t, 51f, 53t; net of student aid, 52–57, 53t, 82; for out-of-state students, 53n65, 89–90; paying for, 6–8, 24; at private universities, 48–50, 50n61; at public universities, 50, 53n65, 78, 87, 88–89n14, 89–90, 106–7; relationship to time-to-degree, 32, 89–90; resistance to increases in, 63; as share of revenues, 78; state funding trends and, 78–79, 79f; trends in, 48–50, 49t, 51f, 107. *See also* affordability; costs of higher education

Turner, Nicholas, 36n45

Turner, Sarah E., 5, 5n5, 19n13, 28,
28n31, 31n37, 32–33, 32n39,
33nn40–43, 42n51, 86, 124
two-year colleges: BA completion rates
of students in, 25, 26, 43, 91;
completion rates of, 22, 86; earnings
of graduates of, 21; effectiveness of,
86, 91; enrollments of, 18, 26n27,
54n66; free tuition at, 26, 90n18, 91;
per-student expenditures at, 107;
remedial courses in, 30–31, 86;
student debt at, 55; tuition costs of,
50; vocational programs of, 20–21

United Kingdom: educational attainment
in, 13; tuition costs in, 87–88
University of Alabama, 121
University of Illinois at Urbana-Cham-
paign, 64
University of Illinois regents, 121
University of Maryland, 124, 133
University of Michigan, 124
University of Wisconsin, 84, 95, 139
University System of Maryland, 127–28
US News ratings, 95–96, 136–37

Vaness, David J., 84n10
veterans, 24, 101n32. *See also* GI Bill
Virginia: attorney general, 65; college completion rates in, 43–44;
higher education costs in, ix,
43–44, 56–57; student database
of, 44n52

Walker, Scott, 84, 139
War on Poverty, 92
Weissman, Jordan, 60n78
White, Dan, 83n8
Wisconsin state government. *See*
Walker, Scott
Woodhouse, Kellie, 2n1, 46n57, 95n25
Wu, D. Derek, ix–xn1

Xu, Di, 130n69

Yale University, 76n3
Yannelis, Constantine, 58–59
Yuchtman, Noam, 130n68

Zakaria, Fareed, 20, 20n16, 21
Zimmerman, Seth D., 26n26, 28